LEADERSHIP GEMS IN THE BIBLE
(THE NEW TESTAMENT)

Also by Chris Omoijiade

THE IRREFUTABLE ROLE OF
GATEKEEPERS TO YOUR SUCCESS
AND HOW TO WIN THEM OVER

YOU TOO CAN BE DEBT-FREE

SO YOU WANT TO LEAD

LEADERSHIP GEMS IN THE BIBLE
(The Old Testament)

GET AHEAD

LEADERSHIP GEMS IN THE BIBLE

THE NEW TESTAMENT

CHRIS OMOIJIADE

Scribe Tribe
www.scribetribe.media

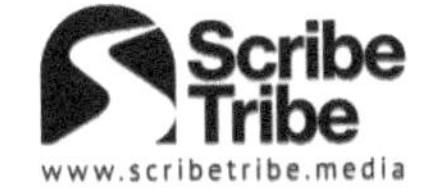

LEADERSHIP GEMS IN THE BIBLE:
The New Testament

Published by:
ScribeTribe Africa
The Scribe Place,
Brownstone Estate,
Lekki, Lagos

www.scribetribe.media
scribetribeafrica@gmail.com
+234 708 040 1080, +234 813 527 3602

Distributed by:
The Chris Omoijiade Company
+234 810 950 0000, +234 908 123 0000
ceo@tcocglobal.com
admin@tcocglobal.com
www.tcocglobal.com
chrisomoijiade
Chris Omoijiade
Christopher Omoijiade
Christopher Omoijiade

THE
Chris Omoijiade
COMPANY
SOLI DEO GLORIA

CHRISTOPHER E. OMOIJIADE
SOLI DEO GLORIA

ARIMATHEA
ARIMATHEA BELIEVERS NETWORK

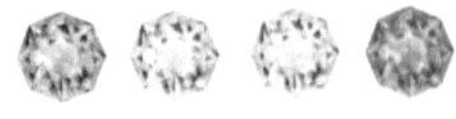

*This book is dedicated to Yahweh,
the I Am, the Holy Father of all spirits
and heavenly lights.*

*To Jesus the Christ, Prince of Peace,
the Word and Eternal King.*

*And the indispensable
Sceptre of the living Sovereign God,
Spirit of Glory, Wisdom and Revelation,
the Holy Spirit.*

*I am indeed a product of
undeserved mercy.*

*Thank you, Abba, for
adopting me!*

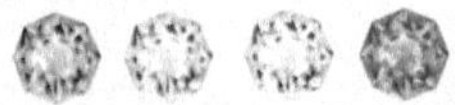

CONTENTS

MATTHEW

Testing God 3

Worship 4

Political Mood 5

Directness 7

The Beatitudes 9

Salt and Light 11

Cut It Off 13

Yes or No Will Suffice 14

Love for One's Enemies 15

Giving to the Needy in a Godly Manner 16

God's Will 17

Treasure 18

God or Mammon 20

Worry 21

Judging Rightly 23

Hypocrisy 24

Selective Giving 26

Do What You Would Like to Receive 27

Build Your Leadership House on the Rock 28

Faith 29

Rejection 31

Where and Who are You Called To? 32

Pray for Others 33

Authority to Those Called 34

The Location of Operation 35

The Opposition 37

Acknowledge God 38

Take Up Your Cross 39

Results Should Do the Speaking 41

Division 42

What is Stored Up in You? 43

Mission Focus 45

Simplifying His Purpose through Parables 46

This Tough Decision 47

No Honour 49

Solitariness 50

Care 51

Plug Wastage 53

Being Quick to Rebuke 54

Inner Circle 55

Leaders are Under the Law 56

Child-Teachability Index 57

Every Follower Matters 58

Negotiate Before Assignments 60

A Hard Cup to Drink 61

Servant First 63

Lowly to be Exalted 64

Who Owns What? 66

TABLE OF CONTENTS

The Greatest Commandment 67

Hypocrisy 69

The Protection of Mother Hen 70

Leaders Always Have Oil 71

ROI Consciousness 72

Betrayal 74

Prepare for Denials 75

Pray to Match Temptations 77

No False Evidence 78

Know When to Speak and When to be Silent 79

Suffering 81

Strategic Relationships 82

Continuity of the Vision 84

MARK

Skepticism 89

Don't Be Surprised by the Alliance of Strange Bedfellows 90

Hope Merchant 91

Organizational Ability 92

Defilement Coming Out of You 93

External Negative Influence 94

Take Time Out to Teach Your Leaders 95

Leaders are Not Fearful of Other Leaders 96

Subordinates Jostling 98

Unpopular Decisions 99

LUKE

Keep Your Own Account 103
Train the Little Ones to Start Early 104
Never Outshine the Master 105
What is Written of You 106
Don't Be Blind 107
Rule Making 108
Private Words 109
Abundance of Possessions 110
All Shall be Added 111
Train the Little Ones to Start Early 112
Decorum in Public Places 113
Project Financing 114
Occupy Till I Come 116

JOHN

Leaders Make Themselves Available 119
Leaders Don't Discriminate 120
Like God, Leaders Must Keep Working 121
Avoid Glory Hunting 122
Premature Assertion To Authority 123
You Will Be Deserted 124
Leaders Don't Follow the Mob 125
The Voice of Leadership 126
Bringing All Under Your Leadership 127
Empathy 128

ACTS

No Gap in Leadership 131

Honour Gives You a Voice 132

Responsibilities 133

The Spirit and Wisdom 133

Stick to Core Functions 134

The Best Talent can be in the Kitchen 135

Speech and Action 136

The Wrong Conviction 137

Learn to Ascribe Praise to God Alone 138

Be Wary of Misleading Advisers 140

Prepare Your Lieutenants from Inevitable Hostility 141

Scrutiny 142

Earning a Living 143

Encouraging Leaders and Converts 144

Be Ready for Debates 145

Language is a Connector 147

Think on Your Feet 148

A Clear Conscience 149

Kick against the Goads 151

Encouragement amidst Hopelessness 152

ROMANS

Constant Intercession 157

Kindness and Sternness 158

Mind Transformation 159

Beware of Pride 160
Love in Action 161
Switch Accordingly 162
Avoid Cursing 163
Harmonious Living 164
Overcoming Evil with Good 165
Peace 166
Revenge 167
All Authority is From God 168
Do Good Towards Those in Authority 169
Pay Your Dues 170
The Only Debt is Love 171
Be Careful of Judgement 172

I CORINTHIANS

Boast Only in God 175
Your Audience Determines Your Delivery 176
Worldly Wisdom 178
Trust and Faithfulness 179
Endurance 180
Benefits 181
Self-Discipline 182
The Dynamics of Temptation 183
Gifts for the Common Good 185
Bad Company 186

TABLE OF CONTENTS

II CORINTHIANS

Your People are the Evidence of Your Workmanship 191
Chastisement 192
Administering Free-Will Giving 193
Witnessed 194

GALATIANS

Bear the Burdens of Others 199
Test Your Actions 200
Sowing and Reaping 201

EPHESIANS

Do Not be Weary in Doing Good 202
Spiritual Blessings 205
Avoiding Falsehood 206
Managing Offences 207
Avoid Stealing 208
Unwholesome Talk 209
Cleanse Your Spirit 210
Expose Evil 211
Live Wisely 212
His Will 213
Honour and Submission 215
The Armour of God 217

PHILIPPIANS

Avoid Grumbling 221

Forget the Past 222

Gentleness 223

Anxiety 224

Meditation 225

Practice 226

The Secret of Contentment 227

COLOSSIANS

Worldly Philosophy 231

Heavenly Perspectives 232

Fairness 233

Handling Outsiders 234

Conversations 235

I THESSALONIANS

Leading a Quiet Life 239

Acknowledging Hard Workers 240

II THESSALONIANS

Deal Decisively with Indolence 243

TABLE OF CONTENTS

I TIMOTHY

Prayer For Leaders 247
What Leaders can Learn from Deacons 248
Godliness 250
Age 251
Watch Your Life 252
Demographics 253
Who's Worse than an Infidel? 254
Contentment 255
Guard What is in Your Care 256

II TIMOTHY

Loyalty and Disloyalty 261
The Victor's Crown 262
Special Purposes 263
Avoid Foolish and Stupid Arguments 264
Persecution is a Necessity 265
Scripture is a Map 266

TITUS

Divisiveness 269

PHILEMON

Forgiveness 273

HEBREWS

Maximizing the Word 277

Mercy and Grace 278

Dealing Gently 279

God's Will 280

Faith 281

Weight and Sin 282

You Have a Precedent 284

Rebuke and Discipline 285

Honourable Living 286

JAMES

The Result of Tests 289

Wisdom can be Sought 290

The Source of Temptation 291

Tame Your Emotions 292

Favouritism 293

Tame Your Tongue 294

Selfish Ambition 295

The Source of Fights and Quarrels 296

Friendship with the World 297

Avoid Slander and Judgement 298

Boasting 300

Rich Oppressors 301

Avoid Swearing 302

Trouble and Happiness 303

TABLE OF CONTENTS

I PETER

Reverent Fear 307

Rid Yourself of Gremlins 308

Inner Beauty 309

Your Gifts are for Service 310

II PETER

Be Alert and Sober 311

Growing in Knowledge 315

What Has Mastered You 317

I JOHN

Love Not the World 321

REVELATION

Leaders are Accountable 325

Hostile Environment 326

Leaders Must Not Be Lukewarm 327

Some Revelations are for Personal Consumption 328

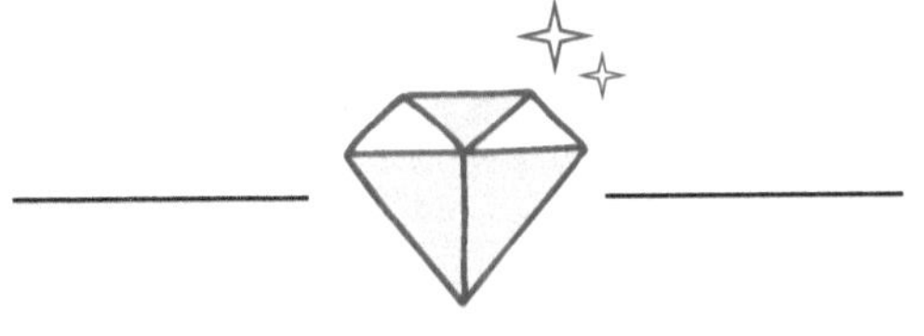

THE BOOK OF
MATTHEW

- ◇ 1 -

TESTING GOD

"Jesus answered him, 'It is also written:
Do not put the Lord your God to the test.'"
Matthew 4:7, NIV

I think even some of the staunchest of believers often forget that Jesus Christ was all God and all Man. When He took on this mortal frame, there was a suspension of His divinity, which did not reduce His leadership standing in the triune God. Yet, He understood and taught earthly leaders why we should not put God to the test. Here was a member of the Godhead being tested by one of His created beings, although a depraved version. Jesus was led by the Spirit into the wilderness to be tempted by the devil; and after a fast spanning forty days and forty nights, He experienced temptations on three occasions.

The tempter understood heaven's hierarchy quite well and, taking Jesus into the holy city, he set Him on the pinnacle of the temple. He quoted Scripture about God's promise to allow His angels to take charge if Jesus cast Himself down. Jesus responded with how wrong it was to test God. In our workings as godly leaders, how many times have we put God to the test? Sadly, some even back their actions with "scriptural references" in order to give credence to their motives.

Whether or not we admit it, putting the Lord to the test will expose us to more temptations and danger. Jesus Christ, when put under the spotlight, gave all godly leaders a pattern to follow. Despite leaving His heavenly position and becoming flesh, He did not tempt God, the Father, and neither should we in our human dealings and affairs.

- ◆ 2 -

WORSHIP

> *"Again, the devil took him to a very high*
> *mountain and showed him all the kingdoms of*
> *the world and their splendor. 'All this I will give you,'*
> *he said, 'if you will bow down and worship me.'*
> *Jesus said to him, 'Away from me, Satan!*
> *For it is written: 'Worship the Lord*
> *your God, and serve him only.'"*
> *Matthew 4:8, 9, NIV*

The devil seeks worship from men, most especially from leaders. He seeks territorial dominance and understands that, while he can chase a million souls, it's a lot easier to corrupt the head. If he can achieve that, it is only a matter of time before the decay of satanic worship seeps through the entire territory, organization or even faith institution. The devil was unrelenting in his intention to outsmart Jesus but, thankfully, the Messiah was equal to the task. He made the devil realize that only God should we worship.

Unfortunately, we live in a world where leaders of various mountains of influence have bitten this bait after they saw the sheer beauty of this temporary earthly plane. They decided to bow their heads to the devil in exchange for short-lived wealth, power and influence. Godly leaders must make a firm covenant to never worship anyone but God. He won't share this space with anyone or anything; therefore, we must be resolute to live by this heavenly expectation.

- ◈ 3 -

POLITICAL MOOD

*"When Jesus heard that John had been put
in prison, he withdrew to Galilee."*
Matthew 4:12, NIV

I have written several leadership articles published across different platforms, and I vividly remember that one of the topics I pondered over was how leadership cannot be divorced from politics. My book "So You Want to Lead" does justice to this assertion. Leaders must understand that man is a political animal; as such, many of our interactions will have political undercurrents whether or not we acknowledge this.

Leaders must learn to read the political mood at any given

time, whether it's in governance, business or even the church. There is always some sort of politicking going on that has a great impact on us as leaders. Jesus Christ, our Symbol of leadership, understood this gem and did just that. John the Baptizer, His cousin, had performed the most important aspect of his ministry by identifying the Saviour, baptizing Him and consequently declaring his own decrease. He would later get into trouble with the authorities, especially with his criticism of King Herod Antipas for marrying his brother's ex-wife, Herodias.

For this reason, he was cast into prison. Jesus, upon hearing this news, promptly withdrew to Galilee. All through His earthly ministry, we are shown the political dexterity of Jesus; He had the ability to read the political mood, and He was so adept at withdrawing from certain territories and locations. Godly leaders must understand the gem of being sensitive to politicking; we must never play ignorantly into a political whirlwind that may have little or no bearing on us.

- ◇ 4 -

DIRECTNESS

"As Jesus was walking beside the Sea of Galilee,
he saw two brothers, Simon called Peter and his brother Andrew.
They were casting a net into the lake, for they were fishermen.
'Come, follow me,' Jesus said, 'and I will send you out to fish
for people.' At once they left their nets and followed him."
Matthew 4:19, NIV

"As Jesus went on from there, he saw a man named Matthew
sitting at the tax collector's booth. 'Follow me,' he told him,
and Matthew got up and followed him."
Matthew 9:9, NIV

Leaders must be direct; they must know what they want without beating around the bush. This is a distinguishing feature of any leader. It reveals his definiteness of purpose. Any leader who is unsure of what to do never truly wins the full respect and admiration of others.

Jesus Christ had done His homework through constant prayer. It was time for Him to start what would be the briefest and yet most important ministry the world would ever see, and He needed men. He understood that, after His death and resurrection, these men would pick up where He would leave off. You will not find a more direct leader like Jesus, as confirmed by His selection process and methodology. It was no guesswork or gamble; He knew the men He wanted and was direct in His instruction towards discipleship.

Beside the Sea of Galilee, we see His first recruitment with the selection of Simon called Peter and his brother Andrew; there is no account of any sweet talking, wooing or cajoling. He knew they had to be part of His world-changing team and would simply say to the fishermen, "Follow me." To establish that this direct method was not a one-off disposition, Jesus also instructed Matthew to follow Him. I am pretty sure the men would have felt something move within them when this direct, life-changing instruction was given. This is because it was far from being a question or request. As Godly leaders, are we direct in our affairs, or do we appear weak, hesitant and uncertain? Leaders are direct and business-like in all their dealings.

- ◈ 5 -

THE BEATITUDES

"Blessed are the meek, for they will inherit the earth."
Matthew 5:5, NIV

"Blessed are the merciful, for they will be shown mercy."
Matthew 5:7, NIV

"Blessed are the pure in heart, for they will see God."
Matthew 5:8, NIV

"Blessed are the peacemakers,
for they will be called children of God."
Matthew 5:9, NIV

"Blessed are those who are persecuted because of
righteousness, for theirs is the kingdom of heaven."
Matthew 5:10, NIV

While growing up, I particularly took a liking to the Beatitudes, maybe because of their simplicity and power. They are a series of blessings pronounced by Jesus in His sermon on the mount. They describe the attitudes and characteristics that are blessed by God and reflect the values of His Kingdom. I have highlighted some which I believe that godly leaders should take cognizance of. The first talks about the meek and the promise of their inheritance of the earth. Leaders are to embody meekness which is a combination of righteousness, humility and patience. This reflects a quality of heart that submits to the will and desire of God.

The second part talks about the blessing that comes to those who are merciful, affirming that they will receive the very same thing they dish out. Leaders must have compassion and extend forgiveness to others, especially those who are under their authority. Several times, we will have to withhold punishment and show lenience.

The third part speaks to the pure in heart, for they will see God. Those who are pure in heart are guiltless, exhibiting integrity at all times. Godly leaders must possess this trait, thus displaying honesty in their intentions, in order to really behold the beauty of God.

The fourth part talks about the peacemakers, for they will be called the children of God. Many leaders profess to be children of God, yet they are instigators of trouble, strife and disharmony. Quite the contrary, godly leaders should mediate between warring parties, thus being at the forefront of initiating reconciliation. Even when wronged, they seek peace and facilitate harmony.

The last part refers to those who will be persecuted because of righteousness and the reminder that theirs will be the Kingdom of Heaven. Many leaders will face persecution and hostility because of their stance for righteousness-doing what is right even in the face of intense opposition and threat to life. They must be courageous, for a reward comes with it. I highly recommend the gems found in the Beatitudes for every leader.

- 💎 6 -

SALT AND LIGHT

"You are the salt of the earth.
But if the salt loses its saltiness, how can it be
made salty again? It is no longer good for anything,
except to be thrown out and trampled underfoot.
You are the light of the world. A town built on a hill
cannot be hidden. Neither do people light a lamp
and put it under a bowl. Instead they put it on its stand,
and it gives light to everyone in the house. In the same way,
let your light shine before others, that they may see your
good deeds and glorify your Father in heaven."
Matthew 5:13-16, NIV

The subject matter of a believer and, by extension, a leader being the salt and light of the earth is well known to many Christians. It is our earthly standard, and Jesus used the concepts to buttress very serious pointers, which I believe leaders can learn a thing or two from.

Salt is used globally; while it boasts several advantages, two of the most significant ones are preservation and taste, especially when it comes to food. Godly leaders must not lose their preservation effect, ensuring that everybody or everything the Lord has committed to us is handled carefully.

We are also "enhancers", thus ensuring anything that is dull is improved on. When we don't live up to our responsibilities—when we lose what is meant to be our advantage—we will be thrown out and trampled upon by men. Leaders are to be transformative and influential agents in all seasons. Without the salt we offer the world, everything will go on to decay.

The second part is our status as light to the world. Again, the significance of light, even in our times and seasons, is well known. When you are indoors, for instance, darkness is accompanied by so much discomfort, pain and anguish. As light of the world, leaders are supposed to transfer illumination across regions and territories, and we are not meant to be hidden. Jesus speaks about how nobody will light a lamp and put it under a bowl; instead, they put it on a stand so that everyone can benefit from it. We are, therefore, implored to let our light shine before others, as leaders, so that men may see our good deeds and glorify God. The presence of light in darkness is definitely unmistakable. Similarly, our presence everywhere must be distinct and impactful. The gem here is to constantly be reminded of these functions – the heavenly ones set for us. Leaders can achieve this by being Christ focused at all times.

- ◈7 -

CUT IT OFF

*"And if your right hand causes you to stumble,
cut it off and throw it away. It is better for you to lose one part
of your body than for your whole body to go into hell."*
Matthew 5:30, NIV

My earliest interpretation of this verse will, no doubt, leave you in stitches: do you mean Jesus wanted me plucking my eyes out and cutting my limbs? Many of us would enter the pearly gates with no body parts and would need angelic attendants to wheel us in.

That aside, a good interpretation of that verse, especially for leaders, is simply for them to cut off or do away with things that will not serve them well, either in their natural work or spiritual dealings. As leaders, we must keep our urges and desires in check. Sin begins in the innermost chambers of our hearts, and God is seeking godly leaders to appreciate the stakes. Leaders will be faced with amplified temptations, as they can sponsor some excesses that lead to sin.

The metaphors in use refer to various aspects of our lives that might cause us to commit sin. It could be possessions, a hobby or a habit. Godly leaders must take the route of disengaging from activities that will lead to further pain here on earth and even in the great beyond. As forward-thinking individuals, we must not give in to the alluring temptation of enjoying momentary pleasures only. The gem here is for godly leaders to constantly prune their lives as a necessity.

- 💎 8 -

YES OR NO WILL SUFFICE

"All you need to say is simply 'Yes' or 'No';
anything beyond this comes from the evil one."
Matthew 5:37, NIV

It is extremely difficult for many people to simply say YES or NO; they use a barrage of words that often gets them into deeper trouble. Godly leaders must be steps ahead by showing the standard when it comes to replies. We must be ready, without beating about the bush, to say either yes or no to issues that come our way. Jesus admonished that your inability to stick to this will make you a mouthpiece of the devil. If there is a category of individuals who should abide by this gem, it should be leaders whose words are held onto by others. Failure to abide by this will surely lead to a breach of trust.

Jesus Christ understands how we can get so carried away and drawn out by our words, from a place of relative safety.

As such, it is vital to master the ability to say, "Yes, I agree" or "No, I cannot do this." Trying to find middle ground to please the hearer puts us in very unpalatable situations and tends to draw us towards errors and, worse, sin. The gem here is godly leaders should always have their yes or no ready at all times – of course, after careful consideration.

- 💎 9 -

LOVE FOR ONE'S ENEMIES

"But I tell you, love your enemies
and pray for those who persecute you."
Matthew 5:44, NIV

Jesus understood the power of love, for it is capable of neutralizing negativity. We are expected, as leaders, to actively love those who seek our downfall and do good to them.

Human wisdom dictates that we visit evil with evil; while this sounds quite logical, it will result in an endless cycle of hurt. In effect, Jesus Christ affirms that the only way that leaves all parties in a better place is walking in love always, including repaying evil with good.

As leaders, showing genuine acts of love and praying for those who persecute us indicate our resolve to surrender all affairs to God. Only Him knows how to judge issues accordingly. Leaders, love your enemies.

- 💎 10 -

GIVING TO THE NEEDY IN A GODLY MANNER

"Be careful not to practice your righteousness in front of others to be seen by them. If you do, you will have no reward from your Father in heaven. So when you give to the needy, do not announce it with trumpets, as the hypocrites do in the synagogues and on the streets, to be honored by others. Truly I tell you, they have received their reward in full. But when you give to the needy, do not let your left hand know what your right hand is doing, so that your giving may be in secret. Then your Father, who sees what is done in secret, will reward you."
Matthew 6:2, NIV

Jesus Christ epitomized giving to the needy. In fact, I make bold to say that He is the most generous Giver in all of human history because He gave His very life to redeem humanity from eternal damnation. Leaders should emulate Him by giving to those in need. In buttressing this point, we are advised that our giving must be done in a godly manner. The Pharisees and religious leaders of that era were victims of self-righteousness; they behaved in ways unbecoming of leaders.

Even today, we find many leaders who play to the gallery; they practise their righteousness in front of others to win the praise and approval of men. As a consequence, they have no reward from God. Godly leaders are not supposed to make a media circus out of supporting the needy. The acceptable standard for leaders, when giving, is to do so privately, so much so that it can be discerned that you are not trying to court attention. Afterwards, we can rest assured that the Lord will reward us as deemed fit.

The gem here is godly leaders, especially in this digital age, must abide by this timeless principle, and not act according to the worldly patterns when it comes to giving to the needy. Giving must always be done in a godly manner.

- ⬦ 11 -

GOD'S WILL

"Your kingdom come, your will be done,
on earth as it is in heaven."
Matthew 6:10, NIV

Leaders on earth must seek one all-important mandate: for God's Kingdom to come and His will to be done on the earth, even as it is in heaven. There exists a parallel world to our earthly abode, and this is heaven where God presides over the universe in His sovereignty. This is not a democracy but a monarchical system where God is Ruler over all, executing His will with mercy and love like no other. While occupying various roles, leaders must be aware that their desires are secondary to that of the One who deployed them there. God wants the deeds on earth to mirror those of heaven, and this will be done faster and more effectively via leaders.

A leader's responsibility is to first seek out God's will for a territory and, by so doing, walk in it to God's glory and praise. When godly leaders always seek God's will, they are guaranteed of His presence in all matters. He is not a man that he should lie, so He will always watch over His Word to perform the same.

- 💎 12 -

TREASURE

"For where your treasure is,
there your heart will be also."
Matthew 6:21, NIV

We all have treasures. Beyond gold and silver, treasures can be anything or anyone that you attach significant importance to, and you will go to any lengths to protect. This is notable because many leaders have their treasures in wrong places and with the wrong people, and the danger here is that your heart is usually invested in where the treasures are.

For instance, if you invest all your earnings and savings in the stock market, the tendency is that you will constantly keep tabs on the market to check on your portfolio. Or let's assume you become emotionally invested in that handsome young man or beautiful damsel; your heart will naturally gravitate towards them in the course of the day, and you will find yourself investing time and resources in that relationship.

God is calling on us to invest more in heavenly treasures and not be overly focused on the unreliable treasures of the earth. Many leaders have their treasures only on the earth, and we discover when studying history that a lot of the wondrous treasures we read of no longer exist. They have been buried by the sands of time. Thankfully, there are treasures that a leader can work for and which time cannot diminish in any way.

- ◈ 13 -

GOD OR MAMMON

*No one can serve two masters. Either you
will hate the one and love the other, or you will be devoted
to the one and despise the other. You cannot serve
both God and money."*
Matthew 6:24, NIV

There is probably nothing that will take a leader's attention from God than money. Money has been, and will always be, a driving force in the scheme of things. Nothing created by men, I believe, holds the same kind of power to influence a human being. Unfortunately, the devil is using it as a weapon, an idol that many people now bow to.

Leaders, due to their unique positioning in managing men and resources, or the nature of leadership, have a front row seat regarding access to money or unlimited resources. Worryingly, some leaders have bowed to Mammon which also means money, material wealth or any entity that promises wealth; it is also associated with the greedy pursuit of ill-gotten gains.

With a firm picture in our minds, we can now expand our understanding of what Jesus Christ meant and how leaders should walk in that consciousness. He says that no one can serve two masters, resulting in the reality that one cannot serve God and money simultaneously. Godly leaders are not immune to the greed and evil of Mammon. It is possible to love money to the point of removing our gaze from God; and the more we journey down that road, the more we will discover that God cannot be served in an acceptable manner when another idol sits on the throne of our hearts. Leaders must appreciate the profound wisdom in this gem and ensure that the sole position of Lord in our lives must be exclusive to God.

- 💎 14 -

WORRY

"But seek first his kingdom and his righteousness,
and all these things will be given to you as well. Therefore do
not worry about tomorrow, for tomorrow will worry about itself.
Each day has enough trouble of its own."
Matthew 6.33, 34, NIV

Worry is a favourite hobby of some leaders, with desks filled with paperwork and tasks, demands within limited time, plans and projects, and concern for people and life itself. So, unknowingly, worry can creep in and become a leader's co-traveller. However, a word of wisdom is given to us to run by, and that is to seek first God's Kingdom and His righteousness while all the things we desire will be given to us. Also, we are advised not to worry about tomorrow because God will sort it out, even while today's issues are sufficient to consider.

We are, therefore, meant to handle what we can achieve on a daily basis; this is not to say leaders should not plan ahead, but we must never allow the worry of tomorrow and what it brings to overwhelm us and make us impotent to the day we have in front of us. Every day will come with its own twists and turns, its own drama and unexpected outcomes; therefore, we are to handle every single day with the wisdom and empowerment of God, and avoid the temptation to worry about the next day after the present day's task has been executed.

Leaders who have ignored this gem tread the faster route towards wear and tear; unfortunately, some suffer untimely deaths from mental burnout. Your world will always present a reason for you to be worried, but your responsibility as a leader is to channel your energy towards meeting God's expectations of you today. It doesn't make sense to take pills today for tomorrow's headache.

- ◈ 15 -

JUDGING RIGHTLY

"Do not judge, or you too will be judged.
For in the same way you judge others, you will be judged,
and with the measure you use, it will be measured to you."
Matthew 7:1, 2, NIV

Jesus Christ is not against judging; in fact, that is an office He functions in. Instead, He desires that leaders' judgements should be fair, conforming to the acceptable standard. We are not to be hypocrites who apply different standards to others and even to ourselves. Jesus' concern is anchored to how we think and, more importantly, how we treat others. And a likely consequence is that we will be judged in the same manner we have exhibited.

One area of judgement is what I may term the quiet, subtle judgement whose seat is in our hearts; often, we don't allow public access to its legal proceedings. Many leaders give insensitive judgements based on what has already been concluded internally. In acting as a mediator, I always stress that a number of tests can be utilized, and one is to put ourselves in other people's shoes. Upon doing so, rational leaders will realize that their perspective on any given matter will change.

We must do well not to think the worst of fellow leaders and those we lead; many of us judge others based on selected negative events in the lives of others, using the same negative brush to paint them completely. This is unacceptable from forward-thinking, empathetic leaders. Leaders must ensure that the standard they have set for themselves must be applied to others. No more, no less.

- ♦ 16 -

HYPOCRISY

*"You hypocrite, first take the plank out of
your own eye, and then you will see clearly to
remove the speck from your brother's eye."*
Matthew 7:5, NIV

The easiest thing anyone can do is fault-finding; you need no academic qualification or specialized training in order to identify the shortcomings of others. It is a standard default feature of fallen, unregenerate men. When a man is hypocritical, he puts up a false appearance of virtue or religion. In other words, the person may claim or pretend to have certain beliefs about what is right but will behave in a way that contradicts those beliefs.

Some leaders must have, at one point or another, fallen short of this. They set and declare lofty standards in public.

They make far-reaching demands of those they surround themselves with; but once the door is shut, and the window blinds are drawn, they struggle to maintain such ideals. Jesus is displeased with leaders – and everyone – who walk in hypocrisy. They are often quick to notice a tiny speck in the eyes of others, oblivious to the fact that they are walking around with planks in their own eyes.

Hypocritical leaders demand that people should do as they say and not as they do. And the led will leave in droves when they realize they are being taken for granted through hypocritical leadership. It is important that leaders first mirror their expectations of others. It fosters deep-rooted respect and an unrivalled commitment from others. Godly leaders walk the talk and not just talk the talk.

They avoid acts and words that will cast a shadow of hypocrisy, whether publicly or privately. They live up to the beliefs they have propagated; they don't criticize others without subjecting themselves to introspection regarding whether they have similar shortcomings. The gem, here, is to avoid hypocrisy and be truthful to yourself and others at any given time. As a leader, this is how to excel without blemish.

- ◈ 17 -

SELECTIVE GIVING

"Do not give dogs what is sacred; do not throw
your pearls to pigs. If you do, they may trample them
under their feet, and turn and tear you to pieces."
Matthew 7:6, NIV

In teaching, Jesus Christ made it abundantly clear as per how we must be wise when it comes to giving our pearls. I would like to define a pearl as anything of significance, whether it is time, resources, connections, relationships, etc. We have spoken about the generosity expected of leaders and, like most principles, there is always a call for balance.

A godly leader must be discerning about whom to give important aspects of themselves to. The verse above speaks to how we are not to give dogs and pigs things that are sacred; we see how canines and swine have no regard for whatever you may consider precious.

Godly leaders must apply wisdom when it comes to selective giving. You must be careful to give out your invaluable resources to only those who will appreciate and cherish them. This gem will save you from seasons of heartache, frustration and anger.

- 💎 18 -

DO WHAT YOU WOULD
LIKE TO RECEIVE

*"So in everything, do to others what you would have
them do to you, for this sums up the Law and the Prophets."*
Matthew 7:12, NIV

Everyone wants to be treated like royalty, but the reality is that what some of us desire is miles away from what we hand over to others. As a leader, you expect sacrifice, yet you are unwilling to make sacrifices; you expect sincerity, but you are unable to give the same to others. You demand accountability and yet fall short of expectations. You instruct people to adhere to the law, yet you flout the same, portraying yourself not to be bound by its consequences.

When we receive something from others, the first question we should ask is, "Am I doing to them, what they are doing to me?" Everything you demand must first be given, and Jesus emphasized that this sums up all of the Law and the Prophets. We must do to others what we expect of them. This is a straightforward and fair law that must guide a leader in all his dealings with others.

- 💎 19 -

BUILD YOUR LEADERSHIP HOUSE ON THE ROCK

*"Therefore everyone who hears these words
of mine and puts them into practice is like a wise man
who built his house on the rock. The rain came down,
the streams rose, and the winds blew and beat against
that house; yet it did not fall, because it had its foundation
on the rock. But everyone who hears these words of mine
and does not put them into practice is like a foolish man
who built his house on sand. The rain came down,
the streams rose, and the winds blew and beat against
that house, and it fell with a great crash."*
Matthew 7:26, 27, NIV

As leaders, I would like to call what we are constructing a leadership house. The foundations will determine the continuity of the house; therefore, the utmost care must be given to the nature of the foundations. From Genesis to Revelation, we have received countless gems in words that we are meant to put into practice; by so doing, we are systematically building our leadership house on the rock. And when the vicissitudes of life come visiting, our establishments will remain unshakable, not primarily because of the windows, doors, or the structures themselves, but majorly because of the foundations they were constructed upon.

For leaders who despise God's words of wisdom, the vicissitudes of life will lead to their miserable decline. Godly leaders execute undertakings in timely fashion based on the godly leadership information they have received. Kindly take my advice: run with building your leadership house on the rock that never fails.

- 🔷 20 -

FAITH

*"When Jesus had entered Capernaum,
a centurion came to him, asking for help. 'Lord,' he said,
'my servant lies at home paralyzed, suffering terribly.' Jesus said
to him, 'Shall I come and heal him?' The centurion replied, 'Lord,
I do not deserve to have you come under my roof. But just say the
word, and my servant will be healed. For I myself am a man under
authority, with soldiers under me. I tell this one, 'Go,' and he goes;
and that one, 'Come,' and he comes. I say to my servant, 'Do this,'
and he does it.' When Jesus heard this, he was amazed and said to
those following him, 'Truly I tell you, I have not found anyone in
Israel with such great faith.'"*
Matthew 8:7-10, NIV

Leaders should exhibit great faith as well; despite our positions and the trappings of power, Jesus expects us to be leaders driven primarily by faith like the patriarchs. Upon entering Capernaum, Jesus was approached by a centurion who asked for help, stressing how his servant lay at home paralyzed and in deep suffering. The Messiah asked if He should follow him to have the servant healed. And in a self-survey of his spiritual standing, he reckoned his insufficiency to have Jesus under his roof. As such, he believed that a word from Jesus would suffice.

A centurion in the Roman army should have a minimum of 100 men under his command, so he understood the significance of authority. Ultimately, Jesus was amazed by his faith, and his servant eventually got well. Leaders must be men of faith, leading with a belief that transcends human sensibilities. We are to be driven beyond what our human eyes can see and even our mortal minds can comprehend. We are to ascend from impossibility to possibility, just like the centurion did, for the Master to be pleased with us. It is impossible to please Him in the absence of faith in our hearts. Situations will arise, and godly leaders must be equal to the task through faith. In many instances, those who are incapacitated like the bed-ridden servant will experience deliverance through our faith.

The gem here is to have a huge reservoir of faith to draw from, come what may. We should accomplish this, knowing that we serve a God who has invested in our leadership to see all men drawn to Him. One can only imagine the huge testimony that would arise among the men and servants of the centurion. We can't afford to fall short of God's expectation.

- ❖ 21 -

REJECTION

*"Then the whole town went out to meet Jesus.
And when they saw him, they pleaded with him
to leave their region."*
Matthew 8:34, NIV

Rejection is real; maybe you have experienced situations whereby those you were leading rejected you, causing you distress. Well, you are not alone. Jesus was rejected and is still being rejected today. Therefore, find peace and comfort. In whatever setting, there may be a group of people who just don't like you, regardless of how much goodwill you bring.

Even in the church, we find leaders who are rejected constantly. This is a cross all leaders must bear. One would expect that such a notable miracle of casting demons out of two men would bring joy to the region of Gadarenes; instead, the inhabitants pleaded that Jesus should leave their region. There was discontent that led to the rejection of the light that came into their midst.

Godly leaders must brace themselves for the impact of rejection in all its forms. Some people may like you, and others may oppose you outright. Therefore, godly leaders must avoid trying in vain to be loved by everyone. We must, instead, prepare ourselves to manage hurt and rejection while going about doing good. Jesus took no offence and left the region; we should emulate Him by walking in love, no matter what, and quit fighting for acceptance.

- 💎 22 -

WHERE AND WHO ARE YOU CALLED TO?

"On hearing this, Jesus said, 'It is not the healthy who need a doctor, but the sick. But go and learn what this means: 'I desire mercy, not sacrifice.' For I have not come to call the righteous, but sinners.'"
Matthew 9:12, 13, NIV

Everyone, including leaders, has where and who they are called to. Jesus, in His appearance at the temple, found what was written about Him in Isaiah; He knew His assignment and who He was called to without any iota of doubt. Many leaders struggle with making an impact because of their inability to identify where they are called and who they are called to; as such, they are unable to stay grounded.

Jesus sat with publicans and sinners, and was questioned by the Pharisees on why He ate with them. On hearing this, He reminded them He came for sinners, and not the righteous. Godly leader, who are you called to take care of? What is your jurisdiction of operation on the earth?

Any leader who attempts to be everything to everyone will eventually fail; after all, a jack of all trades is a master of none. Therefore, it is paramount, especially at the beginning of your journey, to know where your area of operation is and those you are called to.

- ◆ 23 -

PRAY FOR OTHERS

*"Then he said to his disciples,
'The harvest is plentiful but the workers are few.
Ask the Lord of the harvest, therefore, to send out
workers into his harvest field."*
Matthew 9:37, 38, NIV

Leaders need more leaders to get the job done; any attempt to do it all by yourself will guarantee that the job never gets done. Godly leaders must constantly keep seeking God's face to introduce more leaders to the vineyard. Because the portion of Scripture above was targeted at ensuring more souls are won for God's Kingdom, many may interpret it as a clarion call for only those called to the five-fold church ministry.

Nevertheless, this is equally applicable to leaders; we have a divine mandate to be signposts to the Kingdom, and the harvest is abundant, ready for reaping. Those in the five-fold ministry cannot do it all alone, hence the presence of leaders in the workplace, government, etc.

So long as we cannot achieve God's desire by ourselves, we must call on the Almighty to send more men who are purposeful, God-fearing leaders, while we also play our roles in raising a new generation of such leaders who will go and bring in the harvest.

- 💎 24 -

AUTHORITY TO THOSE CALLED

*"Jesus called his twelve disciples to him
and gave them authority to drive out impure spirits
and to heal every disease and sickness."*
Matthew 10:1, NIV

There is always authority that goes along with being called to a specific office or responsibility; when Jesus called His twelve disciples, He gave them authority to drive out impure spirits and to heal every disease and sickness.

Godly leaders have also been given authority to lead others, although it doesn't necessarily have to be for supernatural works as stated above. Authority is like the gunpowder that makes a gun effective; for effective functioning, every leader must identify their authority Source: God. This strengthens and enables us when leading others.

A leader without authority will only be an individual with just a title and nothing more. Godly leaders must strive for more than an office title or designation, which is one of the weakest forms of leadership identified by leadership experts. You must identify the authority to carry out the demands of leadership.

- ◈ 25 -

THE LOCATION OF OPERATION

"These twelve Jesus sent out with the
following instructions: 'Do not go among
the Gentiles or enter any town of the Samaritans.
Go rather to the lost sheep of Israel.'"
Matthew 10:5, 6, NIV

One of the biggest mistakes you can make, as a leader, is not having a defined primary location of operation. Your ability to streamline who and, secondly, where you are called to lead will make you far more efficient. Sometimes, while burning with zeal, we fall for the illusion that we can operate as leaders in every capacity, in any location and to anyone; the end result is often frustration.

Jesus Christ was direct and specific when speaking to His twelve disciples; He instructed them not to go to the Gentiles or enter any town of the Samaritans. Their sole location of operation was to the Jews. In other words, they were not to concern themselves with other nationalities, tribes or tongues but should confine their location to the twelve tribes of Isreal who had lost their way and who Jesus sought to bring back to the Father.

If the twelve leaders had disobeyed this instruction, they most certainly would have failed in their assignment. Godly leaders, like the disciples, must identify and zero in on their locations of operation. When this is achieved, relevance, ability and impact are amplified. Ultimately, success will be attained. The gem here is that leaders must not be too anxious to apply themselves everywhere. With the help of the Spirit, we are to locate our areas of operation to bring greater success and glory to the Father.

- 💎 26 -

THE OPPOSITION

"I am sending you out like sheep among wolves.
Therefore be as shrewd as snakes and as innocent as doves."
Matthew 10:16, NIV

"Do not be afraid of those who kill the body
but cannot kill the soul. Rather, be afraid of the One
who can destroy both soul and body in hell."
Matthew 10:28, NIV

Opposition is as certain as the North Star. It will come to every leader, and Jesus recognized and prepared His disciples for this. They were innocent sheep, and He understood that the world is hostile towards those who genuinely mean well for others while, unfortunately, it embraces those with ulterior motives.

In analyzing this gem, Jesus used two animals to figuratively express the nature of the opposition to His disciples. First, He likened the disciples to sheep, animals that symbolize meekness, purity and innocence. On the other hand, He was sending them among wolves, smart and ravenous animals whose only desire is to prey on the sheep. He, therefore, advocated that, while dealing with such an intelligent foe, they must be shrewd like snakes. This means leaders, in all their dealings, are to be prudent and sensible. We must ensure that we don't get taken advantage of. On the other hand, we must be as innocent as doves. We are to live with a good conscience before God and men; our deeds and thoughts must emerge from clean hands and hearts.

Godly leaders must remain vigilant and pure to overcome the opposition they will encounter. This is the only solution to avoid being consumed.

- 💎 27 -

ACKNOWLEDGE GOD

"Whoever acknowledges me before others,
I will also acknowledge before my Father in heaven.
But whoever disowns me before others, I will disown
before my Father in heaven."
Matthew 10:32, 33, NIV

Have you seen leaders who deny Jesus Christ in the open, and maybe in secret, well-guarded places, they accept His lordship? The Messiah, in speaking to all men, talks about how our words and actions must acknowledge Him before everyone. Leaders, due to their elevated platforms, command an unusual influence that God uses to draw men to Him. It is why He is very intentional about whom He gives this level of power and influence to.

Leaders, today, are quick to absorb all the glory for

achievements and great strides; they rely solely on intellect and strength, and fail to acknowledge the One who gives both and much more. Jesus emphasizes that whoever acknowledges Him as the Source, Provider and Enabler will also be acknowledged before His heavenly Father. Whoever does otherwise will definitely be disregarded.

Godly leaders must make it a habit to constantly acknowledge God in deeds and words before men. They must constantly deflect any praise or self-pride regarding what they have achieved or are achieving. They must be wise to acknowledge God's omnipotent, omnipresent and omniscient qualities as the secret, when men ask questions. This keeps us permanently humble and prevents us from being cast away on the day of reckoning.

- ◇ 28 -

TAKE UP YOUR CROSS

*"Whoever does not take up their cross
and follow me is not worthy of me."*
Matthew 10:38, NIV

Leaders must accept that there is a cross to be taken up, especially when you choose to lead in a godly manner that is unfashionable by worldly standards. This cross may signify consecration, great sacrifice, abstinence, purity, earthly loss, criticism, etc.

Everyone walking with Christ, most especially those called to lead, must take up their cross and follow Him. When you disobey this, you are not worthy of Him and won't partake in much more allocated for those who have resolved to please the Master.

When we think of how Jesus' wooden cross attracted scorn and crushed His mortal body, we can only prepare ourselves for our inevitable march to Golgotha. Godly leaders must prepare themselves to take up their cross; this is the only way that demonstrates our loyalty to the One who called us to lead.

- ◈ 29 -

RESULTS SHOULD DO THE SPEAKING

*"When John, who was in prison, heard about
the deeds of the Messiah, he sent his disciples to ask him,
'Are you the one who is to come, or should we expect
someone else?' Jesus replied, 'Go back and report to John
what you hear and see: The blind receive sight,
the lame walk, those who have leprosy are cleansed,
the deaf hear, the dead are raised, and the good news
is proclaimed to the poor.'"*
Matthew 11:2-5, NIV

Jesus' ministry was just starting off; the word was travelling far and wide about the young carpenter turned Healer and Prophet. He was stepping into the mould of a Shepherd and Leader of hundreds of followers who latched on to His every word and witnessed the astonishing miracles He did.

At this point, His cousin John was already imprisoned, and he wanted to know if the Saviour had really come. Rather than take offence or roll out His leadership credentials as the Chosen One, He taught His followers how to handle such a situation by allowing the results to do the talking.

Results are powerful; they validate our leadership and accord us respect. Results silence critics and answer pressing questions. The miracles done and the Gospel received were testament to Jesus' leadership; and even though you may not replicate those outstanding, miraculous feats, you can also have achievements under your belt that will eliminate all doubts and silence naysayers.

- 💎 30 -

DIVISION

*"Jesus knew their thoughts and said to them,
'Every kingdom divided against itself will be ruined,
and every city or household divided against
itself will not stand.'"*
Matthew 12:25, NIV

Leaders, hear and learn this: the key to effective leadership is called unity. It is foolishness for any leader to attempt to successfully command individuals and resources to a fixed destination without unity. Division is the number one reason why a lot of leaders struggle; they are leading a disunited group of individuals who have not put pride aside and come together to work towards achieving a common goal. Leading in disunity is like swimming against the tide and will get the swimmer absolutely nowhere while exerting tremendous energy in the process.

False charges were brought against Jesus after He had delivered a man possessed by a demon that made him blind and dumb. When the people saw this, Jesus' background was referenced, and He was accused of working with

Beelzebub to cast out devils. Reading their thoughts, He highlighted the foolishness they displayed by declaring that every kingdom that is divided against itself will be ruined, and every city or household divided against itself will not stand. It is not possible for a godly leader to reach certain heights if he and those he leads are divided; the gem here reveals that it is a function of time before the whole show will come crumbling down.

- 💎 31 -

WHAT IS STORED UP IN YOU?

*"A good man brings good things out of
the good stored up in him, and an evil man brings evil
things out of the evil stored up in him."*
Matthew 12:35, NIV

Nothing probably amplifies what a human carries internally more than leadership. Hence, a leader must subject himself to sufficient introspection regarding the state of his heart, as power and authority will further magnify what such a person possesses.

If a leader is genuinely compassionate, it is inevitable that compassion will be a by-word in his leading. If he is genuinely humble, it will be obvious in his dealings with people and things. If such a leader is humane, his emotional intelligence will be resoundingly commendable. So, the question is this: what is stored inside you before you ascend the leadership ranks? If you are already a leader, what qualities, values and mindsets do you embody?

Examining the aforementioned verse closely shows that sufficient effort has been undertaken by someone to store up either good or evil; this is not something a man suddenly wakes up to find embedded in his heart. Therefore, godly leaders must exercise caution regarding whatever they are storing up inside. They must fill their hearts with goodness, purity and love, as leadership draws from this well from time to time.

Godly leaders must constantly ask themselves the question of what is stored inside of them and not take this for granted; it is an exercise that must be done in the secret before the public adulation and search lights are focused on you. We have cases where leaders suddenly become almost inhumane once they start to lead, and we also see leaders who perform outstandingly well in their offices. Both are a function of what has been stored inside of them. Again, what do you have stored inside of you, which is awaiting manifestation?

- ◈ 32 -

MISSION FOCUS

*"While Jesus was still talking to the crowd,
his mother and brothers stood outside, wanting to
speak to him. Someone told him, 'Your mother and brothers are
standing outside, wanting to speak to you.' He replied to him,
'Who is my mother, and who are my brothers?' Pointing to
his disciples, he said, 'Here are my mother and my brothers.
For whoever does the will of my Father in heaven is
my brother and sister and mother.'"*
Matthew 12:47-50, NIV

If there was any leader who was the most mission-focused in all of the Bible, it most definitely was Jesus the Christ. He knew why He came to the world, and He went about achieving the same within a short timeframe: three and a half years. As a Leader, He was determined not to allow anything to shift His gaze from achieving this singular goal – not even family could change this! Some leaders often give justification to so much that deviate them from their leadership goals; while there is a balance to this, we must understand that the only real way of achieving anything tangible is when we are mission focused. The Messiah had a family that He loved, and several parts of Scripture give substance to this; but, understanding human nature, He wasn't going to let even them get in the way of His set goal and agenda.

From Scripture above, we can discern that He was mission conscious; in fact, He affirmed that priority will be accorded to anyone who is really propelled by what needs to be done to please the Father; such an individual will have an enviable ranking in His eyes. This buttresses the importance He placed on doing the Father's will.

Godly leaders, with the help of the Holy Spirit, must be guided in their leadership to remain mission conscious and to also seek men who equally share the same level of passion to deliver on whatever mandate that should be achieved.

- ◈ 33 -

SIMPLIFYING HIS PURPOSE THROUGH PARABLES

"The disciples came to him and asked,
'Why do you speak to the people in parables?'
He replied, 'Because the knowledge of the secrets of
the kingdom of heaven has been given to you,
but not to them.'"
Matthew 13:10, 11, NIV

Sometimes, it's very difficult for leaders to clearly articulate their hearts' desires, and this miscommunication can lead to a disagreement and lack of desired results in the long run. Jesus simplified the communication of His purpose through the use of parables, which were stories used to convey moral or spiritual lessons. In other words, He utilized the ancient art of storytelling to communicate. As a leader, you must be able to ascertain the most favourable method of communication and communicate effectively with the led.

Downplaying this gem will leave your vision in jeopardy. It is your duty to ensure that the vision you carry is well understood by those who are tasked with execution; anything short of this is a crisis waiting to happen. Godly leaders can employ creative means to communicate their agenda so that even a child is able to assimilate it and execute the same accordingly. That should be the uncompromised standard.

- ◇ 34 -

THIS TOUGH DECISION

*"'No,' he answered, 'because while you are
pulling the weeds, you may uproot the wheat with them.
Let both grow together until the harvest. At that time
I will tell the harvesters: First collect the weeds and tie them
in bundles to be burned; then gather the wheat
and bring it into my barn.'"*
Matthew 13:30, NIV

As a leader, you may be faced with making some hard, inevitable decisions. In the process of making such a decision—which is ultimately for the common good—people may have to endure some hardship you would have loved to prevent. It could be that serious. Even Heaven was confronted with such a situation as revealed in Scripture above.

Jesus, never one to shy away from making hard decisions, mentioned that both wheat and weeds should be allowed to grow together until harvest time. This tough decision would mean that both wheat and weeds would compete for space and resources. In other words, there will be some level of discomfort as experienced between believers and unbelievers today.

Godly leaders will have all shades of hard decisions to make and must prepare themselves to deploy divine wisdom in making the right call from tough choices.

- ◈ 35 -

NO HONOUR

*"And they took offense at him. But Jesus said
to them, 'A prophet is not without honor except
in his own town and in his own home.' And he did not do
many miracles there because of their lack of faith."*
Matthew 13:57, 58, NIV

You would think Jesus would have a smooth sail when He declared Himself as Saviour, but He also faced rejection and lack of honour, something all too familiar for leaders. He was in His own country, not a foreign land, and taught them in the synagogue; and they were astonished at the level of His wisdom and mighty works. They then referenced His humble background and pointed out His family members in an attempt to belittle His uncommon deeds.

As expected, Jesus would lay the marker for leaders by reminding them that they may receive no honour in their localities due to familiarity. Godly leaders sometimes endure such dishonour within family circles, among colleagues, etc., but they shouldn't be discouraged. If Jesus encountered contempt in the very place He should have been celebrated the most, chances are that you will endure the same as you attain loftier heights.

- 💎 36 -

SOLITARINESS

"When Jesus heard what had happened,
he withdrew by boat privately to a solitary place.
Hearing of this, the crowds followed him on
foot from the towns."
Matthew 14:13, NIV

Taking time out to be alone is one of the wisest things you can ever do for yourself and leadership. We often run with the assumption that, without us, nothing can work. A leader has failed when they cannot establish systems and structures managed by competent individuals so that you can occasionally take a retreat. It is not compulsory that you should be heard and seen at all times. Therefore, it is critical to know that you might have to withdraw from the limelight sometimes to pray, reflect and get a grip of your emotions.

Jesus greatly utilized this gem; He didn't hesitate to isolate Himself if need be. I make bold to say a leader will discover himself more in those times that in the company of others. John the Baptizer, the great forerunner, had been thrown into jail by Herod; and when his daughter Herodias danced and pleased the king, he made a promise to grant her whatever she wanted. Instructed by her mother, she asked for John's head.

The king, unable to take back his word, acceded to the request. John's head was delivered to the damsel who presented it to her mother. When Jesus heard, He immediately withdrew; of course, Scripture doesn't tell us whether He did that to mourn His cousin, but we can tell that this action was not a one-off event. It was a constant leadership action He took. Little wonder He could commune with His Father and stay the course.

Godly leaders must not run themselves to the ground; they must be wise enough to allocate time and resources to solitary getaways. It will do you a world of good and make you a more effective leader.

- ◈ 37 -

CARE

*"As evening approached, the disciples came
to him and said, 'This is a remote place, and it's
already getting late. Send the crowds away, so they can go
to the villages and buy themselves some food.' Jesus replied, '
They do not need to go away. You give them
something to eat.'"*
Matthew 14:16, NIV

Jesus displayed unrivalled care. Managing the sheer number of people who followed Him from place to place would require great compassion. During one of those episodes, His disciples gauged the atmosphere and informed Him about how far flung they were from civilization, underlining the importance of sending the people away to get food. This could be considered the easiest and most appropriate step to take, considering the circumstances. Where would He get the resources to feed such a large multitude? But even in that dire situation, Jesus showed empathy and care to others by instructing His disciples not to send the people away and, instead, get them something to eat.

This instruction led to one of the most memorable miracles of the ministry of Jesus Christ—feeding five thousand people with five loaves and two fish. As a godly leader, how much do you care for others? Are you so detached that you are unable to connect to people's needs? Or are there certain steps that you can take, which confirm your being God's representative on the earth? Leaders who last are leaders who care. The famous words of John Maxwell rings true: people don't care how much you know, until they know how much you care.

- ◈ 38 -

PLUG WASTAGE

*"They all ate and were satisfied. Afterward the disciples
picked up seven basketfuls of broken pieces that were left over."*
Matthew 14:20, NIV

*"They all ate and were satisfied. Afterward the disciples
picked up seven basketfuls of broken pieces that were left over."*
Matthew 15:37, NIV

Wastage is an act that a leader must frown on. After the multiplication of the bread and fish among five thousand hungry people, we see a repeat of the miracle in the feeding of four thousand people. This time around, He would take seven loaves and fish to fill up the people. Beyond the miracles, His approach towards wastage is worthy of emulation. Many assume that a leader's task is exclusively centered around managing people, not resources.

A leader must constantly manage his resources, or he will eventually run into trouble. Jesus Christ showed His care for resources by plugging wastage: in the first and second miracles, there were twelve basketfuls and seven basketfuls of leftovers respectively.

Leaders are accountable for both people and resources. As a godly leader, you must never encourage or tolerate waste in any form; God hates wastage and so should we.

- 💎 39 -

BEING QUICK TO REBUKE

*"Peter took him aside and began to rebuke him.
'Never, Lord!' he said. 'This shall never happen to you!'
Jesus turned and said to Peter, 'Get behind me, Satan!
You are a stumbling block to me; you do not have in mind
the concerns of God, but merely human concerns.'"
Matthew 16:23, NIV*

A leader's timing of a rebuke is important; there are times when such a rebuke should be done in private; at other times, it must be done in public. Each must be weighed based on the circumstance, the individual, the event and the act eliciting the rebuke.

A godly leader must know how to correct the led accordingly. Jesus, like I indicated earlier, was mission conscious and knew what had to be done to fulfil His mandate on the earth; He had to die gruesomely for the salvation of mankind, and preceding that would mean having to suffer many things in the hands of the Jewish leaders and the Roman authorities. He had started preparing the minds of His disciples about the elders, chief priests and scribes, and how He would die and rise after three days. Peter took Him aside and rebuked Him publicly – something that must never be condoned by a leader from any of his followers.

Of course, Jesus gave him a fitting response! Jesus understood that Peter's statement could have negative effects on the other leaders who looked up to Peter. Therefore, there was a need for an instant public rebuke. The gem here is that a leader must prepare himself to do what is necessary on the spot. This includes either a private or public rebuke depending on the factors I stated earlier.

- 💎 40 -

INNER CIRCLE

*"After six days Jesus took with him Peter,
James and John the brother of James, and led them
up a high mountain by themselves."*
Matthew 17:1, NIV

Leaders are projected to be supermen who are self-sufficient and need no support. In reality, however, even the strongest of leaders need shoulders to lean on; they need those they can trust with their innermost secrets, concerns, plans and even fears. Jesus was no exception despite being the blend of divinity and humanity. He needed close associates that would journey with, and be loyal to, Him on the path to fulfilling His ministry.

If you go through Scripture, you can tell Jesus loved His disciples but had an exceptional fondness for those in His inner circle: Peter, James and John. These men saw Him up close; they were also present during some of His most important events such as the visitation of Elijah and Moses to prepare Jesus for His death. They heard the voice of God Almighty as He registered His pleasure in His Son, Jesus.

It is easy for us to construe that Jesus placed a lot of value on these men and entrusted them with secrets such as the Transfiguration. Every godly leader must have carefully selected individuals who will form the nucleus of his leadership cabinet. You will draw strength, inspiration and hope from your closest associates in good and bad times.

- 💎 41 -

LEADERS ARE UNDER THE LAW

*"But so that we may not cause offense, go to the lake
and throw out your line. Take the first fish you catch;
open its mouth, and you will find a four-drachma coin.
Take it, and give it to them for my tax and yours."*
Matthew 17:27, NIV

On the very day of writing this gem, I put a call across to a community member to apologize for flouting a regulation and immediately engaged steps to correct it after it had been brought to my attention. Unfortunately, herein lies the problem of many leaders; they fall into the trap of believing they are above the law.

The tax officials had approached Jesus and Peter, requesting tax payment. Rather than excuse Himself, Jesus understood that the laws of the land needed to be obeyed. As such, He instructed His disciple to go to the lake, throw out his line, catch the first fish and open its mouth to find a coin, which was used to offset their tax obligations.

Today, we find even spiritual leaders who act as though they are above the law; that is, they are not living by the standards set by Jesus who humbled Himself under human laws. Godly leaders must exhibit good examples by constantly reinforcing their position under the law. By setting such standards, they draw men unto Godliness.

- ◈ 42 -

CHILD-TEACHABILITY INDEX

*"And he said: 'Truly I tell you, unless you change
and become like little children, you will never enter the
kingdom of heaven. Therefore, whoever takes the lowly
position of this child is the greatest in the kingdom
of heaven. And whoever welcomes one such child
in my name welcomes me.'"*
Matthew 18:3-5, NIV

Jesus loves little children for a good reason: they are the most teachable category of human beings; they possess a high score on the teachability index. The teachability index is a measure of an individual's willingness and ability to learn and adapt. This phenomenon is more pronounced in children who are always ready to learn or acquire a new skill.

Interestingly, this is expected of all believers, especially leaders. It is for this reason that Jesus said unless we change and become so humble like little children, we will never enter the Kingdom of Heaven. The lowly position of a child must be the posture of a godly leader. I often encourage individuals to make it a lifetime study to closely monitor children and their attributes. When leaders adopt this position, they put themselves in line to remain humble, amiable, teachable and attractive to others.

- 💎 43 -

EVERY FOLLOWER MATTERS

*"What do you think? If a man owns a
hundred sheep, and one of them wanders away,
will he not leave the ninety-nine on the hills and go to
look for the one that wandered off? And if he finds it,
truly I tell you, he is happier about that one sheep than
about the ninety-nine that did not wander off."*
Matthew 18:12, 13, NIV

What is a leader without a follower? Truth be told, what distinguishes a leader is the influence to get others to follow him or her. And in the analysis of leadership, we will discover that every single follower matters; a number of leaders tend to be carried away by the huge waves of followers, forgetting that every huge number is made up of individual elements. When broken down, every group still boils down to one person. When a leader moves with this perception, they succeed brilliantly.

Jesus showed us the mind of an exemplary leader in this regard; He spoke about how if a man owned a hundred sheep, and one happened to wander away, the shepherd would leave the ninety-nine on the hills and go to look for the one that wandered off. Eventually, he would be happier about that one sheep than the ninety-nine that did not wander. While this parable speaks about God's immeasurable love for a lost soul that is found, godly leaders can also borrow from it to learn about how every single follower is important. Significance must be placed on everyone under your care.

God is intentional down to the smallest numbers. Even when Jesus Christ was giving account to His Father in heaven, in the book of John, we see Him declaring that He kept everyone entrusted to Him, except the son of perdition, so that the Scriptures might be fulfilled. It is a sacred trust God has given leaders over others, and they must lead with the fullest understanding that every single follower matters.

- 💎 44 -

NEGOTIATE BEFORE ASSIGNMENTS

*"But he answered one of them, 'I am not being
unfair to you, friend. Didn't you agree to work for a
denarius? Take your pay and go. I want to give the one who
was hired last the same as I gave you. Don't I have the right
to do what I want with my own money? Or are you
envious because I am generous?'"*
Matthew 20:13-15, NIV

A leader's responsibility may involve having to assign tasks to others, and I have often realized that disregard for this gem can bring disharmony and strife. A leader must learn how to negotiate terms before dishing out assignments. In giving another insightful parable, we see how Jesus speaks of a householder who went out in the morning to hire labourers into his vineyard and was wise to agree with the men he hired at different hours of the day to a particular wage.

At the end of the day, those who were hired much earlier in the day complained of unfairness and disparity in wages, and we see the householder defending his action by asking if the men did not agree to the rates before their work and how he could then be described as being unfair. Again, while this story may have different interpretations, it is important that leaders pick what is relevant to them.

The householder's ability to negotiate with the labourers before dishing out the assignments saved him from embarrassment. We, therefore, must adopt this wise model when it comes to handing assignments to others. Let everything be well spelt out beforehand. Negotiate and reach an agreement before any other thing. Notably, this is applicable to some other areas of life.

- 45 -

A HARD CUP TO DRINK

"'What is it you want?' he asked. She said,
'Grant that one of these two sons of mine may sit at
your right and the other at your left in your kingdom.'
'You don't know what you are asking,' Jesus said to them.
'Can you drink the cup I am going to drink?' 'We can,'
they answered. Jesus said to them, 'You will indeed drink
from my cup, but to sit at my right or left is not for me to
grant. These places belong to those for whom they have
been prepared by my Father.'"
Matthew 20:21-23, NIV

Loftier heights are indeed beckoning to some of us; the only silent words not spoken to those who desire such is that these heights come with a huge price. In whatever sphere of leadership, a huge number of ill-prepared individuals won't see the thorns before the rose; they won't understand there is a hard cup to drink from before ascending the throne.

The mother of James and John had approached Jesus, desiring a favour from the Messiah. She desired that her sons should sit at either side of Jesus at His exalted position in His Kingdom. He responded that that would be possible provided they were prepared to drink from the cup He would drink from. Besides that, the position they sought would be allocated by only the Father.

Godly leaders who aspire to different prestigious positions must appreciate the pattern that there is a bitter cup they will drink from. We should also be reminded that the Father who appoints kings—who is the Governor among the nations—has the sole prerogative of deploying people in different positions, roles or offices.

- 💎 46 -

SERVANT FIRST

*"Jesus called them together and said, 'You know that
the rulers of the Gentiles Lord it over them, and
their high officials exercise authority over them. Not so
with you. Instead, whoever wants to become great among
you must be your servant, and whoever wants to be first
must be your slave—just as the Son of Man did not
come to be served, but to serve, and to give his life
as a ransom for many.'"*
Matthew 20:26-28, NIV

The phrase "servant leader" is now part of popular culture and our lexicon, but it is not a new era invention. It has been in place a long time ago but was made more popular only in recent times. A servant leader prioritizes serving for the greater good. They put others, their team and their organization first, while their own personal needs and objectives become secondary. It is probably the most powerful style of leadership because the individual is a servant first before a leader.

Jesus Christ exemplified this mode of leading. The indignation was evident from the other ten disciples who had heard the ambitious request from the Zebedee household. The Messiah saw it as a perfect time to elaborate on the style of leadership that heaven approved of, speaking about the rulers of the Gentiles.

He reminded them about how these rulers exercised authority without care. He then reminded this new breed of godly leaders that God sought men who desired to first become servants to those they intended to lead. He spoke to the ambition in the hearts of leaders, admitting that anyone who sought to be first must initially take the last position. Commendably, He was practising what He preached because He didn't come to be served, but to serve, thereby giving His life as a ransom for many.

The gem here is that no other style, form or method of leadership has proved to be more impactful and successful; as such, anyone who wants to be a leader of leaders must first be a servant of servants.

- 💎 47 -

LOWLY TO BE EXALTED

"Say to Daughter Zion, 'See, your king comes
to you, gentle and riding on a donkey, and on
a colt, the foal of a donkey.'"
Matthew 21:5, NIV

Leaders are to remain lowly to be exalted just like Jesus Christ. He wasn't on earth to jostle for endorsement or approval ratings; rather, He concentrated on remaining humble only for Him to be ultimately exalted. He was given a place at the right hand of the Father and an unmatched name.

It was time for Him to return to Jerusalem for what is now popularly referred to as His Triumphant Entry. While Jesus rode majestically, He accepted the praise which He did not originally seek. By contrast, some leaders would love to be in the spotlight, receiving praise and acknowledgment at all cost.

They manipulate people and systems to be on the receiving end of recognition and honour. Jesus opted, like all wise leaders, to remain humble, and He was rewarded with exaltation. Nothing is more beautiful to behold than a leader who understands and runs with this gem; remain lowly, and be assured of other men and the Father exalting you in due course.

- 💎 48 -

WHO OWNS WHAT?

*"'Caesar's,' they replied. Then he said to them,
'So give back to Caesar what is Caesar's,
and to God what is God's.'"*
Matthew 22:21, NIV

A clear distinction must be made by leaders on who owns what; there is an allocation that is due to men, and others must be given to God alone. There may be an occasion when some may seek to entangle you with your words and actions in order to find grounds with which to bring down your leadership, and the most sensitive area is in the balance between the state and God. This conversation is not new; leaders will have to navigate their obligations to established earthly authorities and heavenly establishments governed by God.

The Pharisees took counsel and set a trap for Jesus; they sent their agents to make a mischievous enquiry. After paying lip service of honour, they asked if it was lawful to give tribute to Caesar or not. Jesus, perceiving their craftiness, asked why He was being tempted and requested that a tribute coin be brought to him. The image on the coin was Caesar's, and He simply replied to them to give back to Caesar what was his and to God what was God's. This wisdom should be the hallmark of any godly leader, most especially in our modern society that doesn't hesitate to paint Christian leaders in a bad light. Some of such leaders have been persecuted in the sense of being portrayed as guilty of disregarding earthly regulations and laws. Therefore, the gem or timeless wisdom bestowed to us is to simply give people and God what is due them.

- 💎 49 -

THE GREATEST COMMANDMENT

"Jesus replied: 'Love the Lord your God with all
your heart and with all your soul and with all your mind.'
This is the first and greatest commandment. And the second
is like it: 'Love your neighbor as yourself.' All the Law and the
Prophets hang on these two commandments.'"
Matthew 22:37-39, NIV

The greatest commandment that was emphasized by Jesus Christ to all men, including leaders, sounds very basic and passive, yet it is the hallmark and foundation of our faith. As godly leaders, He tells us that our sole duty is two-fold: one to God and the other to fellow men. Our duty is to love God with all our hearts, souls and minds. We are to hold nothing back regarding our worship of the God of creation; our creativity, our strength, our resources, our time, our will, our intellect and very core must be directed towards loving God, which is the first and greatest commandment.

In other words, this is the most important expectation God looks out for, which should drive us every day.

The second is to love your neighbour as yourself – God expects leaders to love their fellow human beings in the same vein that they like themselves. The fallen human nature is such that we selfishly put ourselves first before others. In contrast, Jesus expects our human relationships to be governed by love and completely rid of selfish intent; we are to treat others as we expect them to act towards us. Love is so compelling that even Jesus affirmed that the Law and the Prophets derived their essence from it. This gem of love towards God, first, then men, next, should be handled with deep reverence for the Almighty, the utmost humility and extreme caution.

- ◈ 50 -

HYPOCRISY

"Everything they do is done for people to see:
They make their phylacteries wide and the tassels on
their garments long; they love the place of honor at
banquets and the most important seats in the synagogues;
they love to be greeted with respect in the marketplaces
and to be called 'Rabbi' by others."
Matthew 23:5-7, NIV

Jesus detested, and still detests, hypocrisy among leaders. Such people love to do stuff merely to curry favour or for the accolades of men. I remember once receiving an instruction from the Lord to never seek out the praise of men; God elevates and keeps in authority men who shun hypocrisy of every kind.

The Jewish leaders, during the time of Jesus, were well versed in the laws of Moses, and they commanded so much respect among the children of Israel. Over time, pride crept in, and they soon began to exhibit hypocritical tendencies. Their actions were men focused, not God focused. Their phylacteries (small leather boxes containing the Hebrew texts, which were used at morning prayers as a reminder to keep the law), were wide, most likely to court attention. Worse still, they sought the best seats at public forums and in the synagogues. Finally, they loved to be greeted in the marketplaces with respect and be called teacher by all. All of this was self-centered, not God centered.

Jesus affirmed that leaders should steer clear of the Jewish leaders' disposition. Our public conduct, dressing, etc. must not be targeted at courting human attention, causing men to shift their gaze from God to us.

- 💎 51 -

THE PROTECTION OF MOTHER HEN

*"Jerusalem, Jerusalem, you who kill the prophets
and stone those sent to you, how often I have longed
to gather your children together, as a hen gathers her
chicks under her wings, and you were not willing."*
Matthew 23:37, NIV

Mother hens are often viewed as protective, quick and authoritative. At all costs, their aim is to give emotional and physical security to their chicks, even to the extent that they can be aggressive towards the chicks of another mother hen.

During Jesus' triumphant entry into the city of David, the historical record of how the city had killed her prophets sent by God was laid bare. Jesus then went on to express His longing to have the people of Jerusalem submit to the security and guidance that only Him could offer, despite their unwillingness.

Leaders should seek to be like the mother hen; we should offer protection and provision to those under our care, as the Lord has empowered us. God didn't accidentally deploy us in those strategic leadership positions. Indeed, we were born for a time as this.

- ◇ 52-

LEADERS ALWAYS HAVE OIL

"Five of them were foolish and five were wise.
The foolish ones took their lamps but did not take
any oil with them. The wise ones, however, took oil
in jars along with their lamps."
Matthew 25:2, 3, NIV

Leaders are intentional people. They should never be found unprepared. One of the benefits godly leaders enjoy is walking with the Holy Spirit who helps us to constantly be in the mood of preparation.

In the narrative above, Jesus stressed the wisdom of five virgins and the foolishness of the other five, due to preparation or lack of it. Because the foolish ones couldn't get oil from the wise virgins, they left to purchase oil at the wrong time. Sadly, on their return, they were shut out of the marriage ceremony.

Leaders shouldn't be caught unawares. They should constantly have the resources to alleviate any unpleasant surprises. What is more, God expects leaders to always have oil in anticipation of His return.

- ◇ 53 -

ROI CONSCIOUSNESS

"His master replied, 'You wicked, lazy servant!
So you knew that I harvest where I have not sown
and gather where I have not scattered seed? Well then,
you should have put my money on deposit with the bankers,
so that when I returned I would have received it back
with interest. So take the bag of gold from him and give it
to the one who has ten bags. For whoever has will
be given more, and they will have an abundance.
Whoever does not have, even what they
have will be taken from them."
Matthew 25:27, 28, NIV

Although the parable of the talents means different things to various commentators, I seek to absorb the leadership lesson embedded in it. In this narrative, a master who embarked on a journey later discovered, upon his return, that the first servant who was given five talents had made a profit of another five talents. The second servant added two talents to the original two he was given. Mark you, this master distributed the talents among his three servants according to their ability; so, it wasn't an unjust distribution.

Unfortunately, the last servant buried the one talent handed to him. His line of defence was that his lord was a tough man who loved reaping where he had not sown. This master, representing God, spoke back about the wickedness of the servant who was aware of his desire for returns and chastised him for not keeping the money in the bank to gain interest at the very least.

Godly leaders are ROI conscious; therefore, when giving responsibilities and resources at all times, we must remain vigilant about which of our followers can truly appreciate and maximize what has been entrusted to them. God possesses this nature, and so should you. This is why you cannot afford to assign tasks or appoint people on the bases of emotions, tribal inclinations and the like. If anything, competence and integrity must be given the utmost consideration.

- 💎 54 -

BETRAYAL

*"Then one of the Twelve—the one called Judas Iscariot—
went to the chief priests and asked, 'What are you willing
to give me if I deliver him over to you?' So they counted out
for him thirty pieces of silver. From then on Judas watched
for an opportunity to hand him over."*
Matthew 26:15, 16, NIV

Again, the subject matter of betrayal rears its ugly head. Jesus Christ was at the last lap of His earthly ministry, and the Pharisees and Jewish elders had done all they could to penetrate and hold Him culpable for some trumped-up charge. Many leaders are all too familiar with betrayal. They have fallen from great heights only because people in their inner circles sold them out to their enemies.

In the case of Jesus Christ, it was Judas Iscariot, the ministry's treasurer. He betrayed Jesus for thirty pieces of silver, eventually discovered the degree of his evil and committed suicide. In fact, He has become the poster boy for betrayal in Christian circles. The reality is there are still so many people like Judas Isacriot around leaders; you can do all that is expected of you, and it still won't stop them from giving themselves over to be vessels of evil.

A leader, therefore, keeps an eye out and also guards his heart with all diligence in preparation for any eventuality of betrayal.

- ◈ 55 -

PREPARE FOR DENIALS

"'Truly I tell you,' Jesus answered, 'this very night,
before the rooster crows, you wilal disown me three times.'
But Peter declared, 'Even if I have to die with you, I will never
disown you.' And all the other disciples said the same."
Matthew 26:34, 35, NIV

Often, the cousin of betrayal is denial; it can hurt just as badly as betrayal. Jesus was speaking to His leaders about an inevitable occurrence in His journey; the end was near, and He would soon be nailed to the cross at Golgotha. When speaking about the troubles that awaited Him, Peter declared that he would stick with Him come what may. I quite honestly believe he genuinely meant it, but he was oblivious of the stretching that was to come.

Jesus Christ, being the ultimate Leader, knew that denials come in the face of severe trials and circumstances. He informed Peter that he would deny his Master three times before the rooster crowed. This unfolded after the mob would come to arrest Jesus. Peter would follow the bloodthirsty mob, while the officials presented Jesus to the authorities. While warming himself at a nearby fire, Peter would find himself confronted by a young slave girl; and after probing his identity as one of the followers of the then accused Christ, Peter would deny his Master three times as Jesus affirmed. Afterwards, he ran off weeping about how he had openly denied the One he had walked with all the while.

Godly leaders like Jesus must never take denials to heart; we must learn to walk in love nonetheless. As Scripture later stated, the resurrected Jesus still sought Peter by the sea despite the denial. A leader will find himself bruised emotionally and weakened mentally if he doesn't embrace this admonition.

– ◈ 56 –

PRAY TO MATCH TEMPTATIONS

*"Watch and pray so that you will not fall into temptation.
The spirit is willing, but the flesh is weak."*
Matthew 26:41, NIV

*"Very early in the morning,
while it was still dark, Jesus got up, left the house a
nd went off to a solitary place, where he prayed."*
Mark 1:35, NIV

A leader faces a barrage of temptations, many of which are never made public. Jesus understood that the only real strategy that a godly leader possesses to match up to the schemes of this world is to watch and pray. Jesus Christ explained to the leaders that they must spend time in being watchful; in other words, leaders are to be watchmen who are cautious about what seeks to take them down. The second strategy is prayer.

Jesus also demonstrated how leaders should overcome the weakness of the flesh, thus latching on to the willingness and strength of the spirit, by arising very early in the morning and spending considerable time to pray in a solitary place. This strategy was enough to ward off the temptation that was already prepared for the day.

A leader who attempts to fight off the temptations connected to their office, by other means, will definitely fail. Your leadership journey must be governed by watchfulness and prayer if you truly desire to stay grounded.

- ◈ 57 -

NO FALSE EVIDENCE

"The chief priests and the whole Sanhedrin
were looking for false evidence against Jesus
so that they could put him to death."
Matthew 26:59, NIV

Enemies of leaders are constantly in the business of gathering intel on leaders; we see, in our modern political space, how dirt is constantly being archived and later thrown in the faces of unsuspecting leaders. A godly leader must, therefore, ensure that no false evidence can be gathered against them. Even if such is attempted, God will surely vindicate you as long as it isn't true.

In Scripture above, we can see how the chief priests and the whole Sanhedrin were looking for false evidence against Jesus so that they could put Him to death. Leaders will be tested and tried, but they must be steadfast about living a life of integrity and blamelessness like Jesus. Eventually, whatever trumped-up charge the enemies bring against you will be proved otherwise, and God will be glorified. This gem should forever be treasured.

- 💎 58 -

KNOW WHEN TO SPEAK AND WHEN TO BE SILENT

*"Then the high priest stood up and said to Jesus,
'Are you not going to answer? What is this testimony
that these men are bringing against you?' But Jesus
remained silent. The high priest said to him, 'I charge you
under oath by the living God: Tell us if you are the Messiah,
the Son of God.' 'You have said so,' Jesus replied. 'But I say
to all of you: From now on you will see the Son of Man
sitting at the right hand of the Mighty One and
coming on the clouds of heaven.'"*
Matthew 26:63, 64, NIV

*"Meanwhile Jesus stood before the governor,
and the governor asked him, 'Are you the king of
the Jews?' 'You have said so,' Jesus replied. When he was
accused by the chief priests and the elders, he gave no answer.
Then Pilate asked him, 'Don't you hear the testimony
they are bringing against you?' But Jesus made no reply,
not even to a single charge—to the great
amazement of the governor."*
Matthew 27.11-14, NIV

It is important that a leader should know when to speak and when to be silent. We must be careful because our words might be manipulated by mischievous folks but, often, silence can't be quoted. I personally live by the code of assumption that everything I say in private could be made public, and this includes everything I write in this social media conscious generation. The wisdom of utterance or the lack of it is important for a godly leader.

Jesus was before the leadership hierarchy, and the High Priest stood up and asked whether He would respond to the accusation against Him, but He remained silent. When the high priest, under oath by the living God, enquired if He was the Messiah, He said, "You have said so." That was a wise, sharp and swift response. After that, He declared His divinity in the hearing of everyone. In another episode, He simply said, "You have said so" when the governor asked if He was the King of the Jews. However, when the chief priests and elders accused Him, He kept quiet yet again.

Jesus, by the help of the Spirit, taught us that there is indeed a time to speak and a time to be silent; wise leaders abide by this rule of operation, and so should you.

- 💎 59 -

SUFFERING

*"Then the governor's soldiers took Jesus into the
Praetorium and gathered the whole company of soldiers
around him. They stripped him and put a scarlet robe on him,
and then twisted together a crown of thorns and set it on
his head. They put a staff in his right hand. Then they knelt
in front of him and mocked him. 'Hail, king of the Jews!'
they said. They spit on him, and took the staff and struck
him on the head again and again. After they had
mocked him, they took off the robe and
put his own clothes on him. Then they led
him away to crucify him."*
Matthew 27:31, NIV

A leader's suffering comes in different shades, sometimes
ending in gory deaths and destruction. There could be
seasons of great suffering because of the path you have
chosen to tread as a righteous leader. Jesus understood
this and prepared Himself at the garden of Gethsemane;
eventually, He was comforted by angels.

After Jesus' arrest, He was led away, and judgement was
passed on Him. At the Praetorium, the official residence of
the Roman Governor, the governor's soldiers visited great
suffering on Him, stripping Him, putting a scarlet robe on
Him and setting a painful crown of thorns on His head.
After mockery, He was led away to crucifixion.

While your version of suffering may not be as graphic as the Messiah's, it is important we understand that the huge cost of leading others, in obedience to God's clarion call, entails some suffering that is inevitable.

- 💎 60 -

STRATEGIC RELATIONSHIPS

"As evening approached, there came a rich man from Arimathea, named Joseph, who had himself become a disciple of Jesus. Going to Pilate, he asked for Jesus' body, and Pilate ordered that it be given to him. Joseph took the body, wrapped it in a clean linen cloth, and placed it in his own new tomb that he had cut out of the rock. He rolled a big stone in front of the entrance to the tomb and went away."
Matthew 27:57-60, NIV

The importance of a leader cultivating strategic relationships cannot be overemphasized. Some leaders have left office to no applause, enjoying little or no support after their tenures, because they didn't engage the foregoing reality.

During a leadership tenure, you must build strategic relationships that will support you during and after your leadership; every leader who falls at this hurdle will have no one to blame but himself. The importance of picking and building godly relationships with those who will carry your weight will be revealed at the point of need. Thereafter, you must be open to selecting the right individuals from all walks of life.

After Jesus' death on the Cross, a certain rich man from Arimathea named Joseph—he was Jesus' disciple and definitely commanded some political clout as revealed by his access to Pilate—emerged as the evening approached and requested Jesus' body from Pilate. This was granted, and Joseph ensured Jesus' body was placed in his own tomb.

I am almost certain that Jesus was strategic in the relationships He built, from the disciples He chose, to the women who supported Him in ministry and even those who took care of His body, for the prophecy about His purpose to be fulfilled. Godly leaders must, therefore, be intentional about strategic relationships. The absence of this will fuel a miserable and lonely life, either during or after the time of wielding authority.

- 💎61 -

CONTINUITY OF THE VISION

"Then the eleven disciples went to Galilee,
to the mountain where Jesus had told them to go.
When they saw him, they worshiped him; but some
doubted. Then Jesus came to them and said, 'All authority
in heaven and on earth has been given to me. Therefore go
and make disciples of all nations, baptizing them in the name
of the Father and of the Son and of the Holy Spirit,
and teaching them to obey everything I have
commanded you. And surely I am with you
always, to the very end of the age.'"
Matthew 28:17-20, NIV

A godly leader's vision should never die with him; there are amazing leaders whose visions have evaporated after their demise, with little or nothing for others to build upon. We must work on not only the vision at the time of execution, but also the plan for when you have to pass the baton.

Jesus understood this gem, so He reinforced the vision to His disciples by telling them to go and make disciples of all nations by baptizing them in the name of the Father, the Son and the Holy Spirit, and teaching them everything they had learnt from Him.

A leader must be intentional about having a long-term plan of his vision. The reason you are reading this is that Jesus oversaw the implementation of the long-term goal. In fact, the vision is still profoundly impactful over 2,000 years after it came through His birth.

THE BOOK OF
MARK

- 🔷 62 -

SKEPTICISM

*"The people were all so amazed that they asked each other,
'What is this? A new teaching—and with authority! He even gives
orders to impure spirits and they obey him.' News about him
spread quickly over the whole region of Galilee."*
Mark 1:27, 28, NIV

When an individual is said to be skeptical, he or she doubts the truth. Leaders will also face skepticism about their leadership from some quarters. From experience, I can assure you that not everyone will accept you; though this shouldn't make you doubt that you are in good company.

Even Jesus, in spite of His ministry marked by insightful teachings and astonishing miracles, encountered skepticism. Similarly, you shouldn't be taken aback if your promises, your selection, your vision or plans—all done in a godly manner—are challenged by skepticism. Some will doubt you because they may consider your posture of Godliness as a cover up to perpetrate nefarious activities. This must never deter you from leading people in a manner that is pleasing to God.

- ◈ 63 -

DON'T BE SURPRISED BY THE ALLIANCE OF STRANGE BED FELLOWS

*"Then the Pharisees went out and began to plot
with the Herodians how they might kill Jesus."*
Mark 3:6, NIV

I presume you may have heard the phrase that "The enemy of my enemy is my friend." Therefore, a leader must not be taken aback by the alliance of strange bed fellows who may seek his downfall. A godly leader can be at the receiving end of a conspiracy.

A typical example is the marriage of convenience between the Pharisees and Herodians. The Pharisees formed the strict party of the law in Judea, rejecting and despising all Roman rule and authority, and cooperating to preserve their own position in Israel. Theirs was a temporary arrangement as they looked forward to the coming Messiah and King.

The Herodians, on the other hand, were an official sect containing many Sadducees and scribes, and their hope was based on the house of Herod, the Edomite. Herod had ensured some measure of self-rule, and the Herodians were dedicated to his descendants remaining on the throne. Despite this sharp difference, the two sects had a mutual enemy called Jesus Christ. They knew they would be in trouble if Jesus' influence was left unchecked.

This spectacle reveals that humans can go to any lengths to silence anyone or anything that challenges their self-interest. Godly leaders must be wary of such alliances orchestrated for their downfall because they are considered threats.

- ◈ 64 -

HOPE MERCHANT

*"While Jesus was still speaking, some people came
from the house of Jairus, the synagogue leader. 'Your daughter
is dead,' they said. 'Why bother the teacher anymore?'
Overhearing what they said, Jesus told him,
'Don't be afraid; just believe.'"*
Mark 5:36, NIV

A famous leader once said that, "Leaders are dealers in hope." Leaders, as dealers of hope, understand that their actions or words can mean the difference between hanging on or giving up. The moment we are unable to transact in hope, we will lose most, if not all, we stand for.

Rather than sink into misery and tears upon receiving the bad news, Jesus simply dealt in hope for the moment. He told Jarius not to be afraid but to just believe. Afterwards, He would go in the company of Peter, James and John to bring the child from the dead.

Jesus, as a leader, ensured that the key pillars of His team understood the power and importance of a hope merchant. Even in the midst of unpalatable situations—even when your followers or people around you portray worry, doubt or fear—godly leaders must always dispense hope.

- ◈ 65 -

ORGANIZATIONAL ABILITY

*"So they sat down in groups
of hundreds and fifties."*
Mark 6:40, NIV

Some people often assume that organizational ability is a modern-day concept, but that is not the case. In the narrative of the miracle performed to feed the five thousand, we can take our cue from what Jesus did after the disciples had highlighted the problem related to the people's welfare.

Thankfully, a lad had five loaves and two fish which were enough for Jesus to work with. Here comes the gem that leaders should pay attention to: Jesus directed the disciples to have all the people sit down in groups; they did so in groups of hundreds and fifties. Before the miracle was performed, order was instituted.

Godly leaders must never compromise on organization when

leading; they must learn to institute systems that will make for better e<ciency in all of their operations.

- ✦ 66 -

DEFILEMENT COMING OUT OF YOU

*"'Are you so dull?' he asked. 'Don't you see
that nothing that enters a person from the outside can
defile them?' He went on: 'What comes out of a
person is what defiles them.'"*
Mark 7:18-20, NIV

A godly leader, at all times, must walk in and work with the consciousness of how defilement operates in the life of a man. Speaking to the crowd that had gathered, Jesus highlighted the source of defilement which is the act of making something foul or unclean. The devil understands that a defiled leader can produce only rotten fruit that won't improve or transform the lives of others.

Jesus affirmed in clear terms that what emerges from within, from a man's heart—not what goes in—defiles a man. A godly leader must embrace this reality and steer clear of all manner of defilement, including sexual immorality, theft, murder, greed, malice, deceit, lewdness, envy, slander, arrogance and folly.

Whenever any of this begins to rear its ugly head from within, leaders should be sensitive and quick enough to eliminate it from its roots, first, through submission to God via prayer and the Word, and, next, through a change of attitude. Failure to do so will definitely lead to the mismanagement of such a leader's life, as well as the people and resources entrusted to him.

- ◈67 -

EXTERNAL NEGATIVE INFLUENCE

"'Be careful,' Jesus warned them. 'Watch out for
the yeast of the Pharisees and that of Herod.'"
Mark 8:15, NIV

In the hands of a baker, leaven is usually a substance, typically yeast, which causes dough to rise. It can also symbolize something that enlivens or markedly alters the total quality of another thing. It is, therefore, a metaphor for influence and growth.

In the days of Jesus, the yeast of the Pharisees signified corruption. Jesus warned the leaders around Him to be careful of the negative influence of the Pharisees and Herod, which produced undesirable results.

Just like the traditional leaven that alters total quality,

leaders must be wary of, and be swift to eliminate, negative influences that can corrupt them, other people and systems, thus jeopardizing the visions and objectives they set to achieve.

- ◈ 68 -

TAKE TIME OUT TO TEACH YOUR LEADERS

"They left that place and passed through Galilee.
Jesus did not want anyone to know where they were,
because he was teaching his disciples. He said to them,
'The Son of Man is going to be delivered into
the hands of men. They will kill him, and
after three days he will rise.'"
Mark 9:30, 31, NIV

A major part of a leader's responsibility is teaching those they are called to lead. This task must never be left to chance but must be meticulously and methodically planned and executed. A leader must be able to impart sufficient wisdom and knowledge from the bowels of their experience to direct the leaders under them unto the path of Godliness and righteousness.

Jesus demonstrated just this before His death. In fact, He didn't want anyone to know where they were solely because He was teaching His disciples. We see the godly pattern of isolation for effective mentoring. It is noteworthy that many leaders across different spheres implement this in the areas of corporate retreats, etc. This should also be implemented by church leaders in a timely manner to ensure young leaders are well equipped.

The return on investment for such an action is unquantifiable. Replicating your godly values and conduct in others is the greatest achievement of a servant leader and is a precursor to more lasting leadership success. The gem here is if you are a godly leader, you must allot time to engage your followers through deliberation, brainstorming, encouragement, prayer and fellowship with one another.

- ◈ 69 -

LEADERS ARE NOT FEARFUL OF OTHER LEADERS

*"'Teacher,' said John, 'we saw someone driving
out demons in your name and we told him to stop,
because he was not one of us.' 'Do not stop him,'
Jesus said. 'For no one who does a miracle in my name
can in the next moment say anything bad about me,
for whoever is not against us is for us.'"*
Mark 9:38-40, NIV

The fear of someone else taking the shine must never be found in a godly leader; it is a sign of an unregenerate leader who is still walking according to the flesh or the patterns of this world. And the result of such is never palatable. A leader must be confident in himself, his abilities and his gifting, and also be assured in his position.

We see this play out in the life of John the Baptizer, a renowned prophet identified for the singular role of introducing the Lamb who takes away the sins of the world and baptizing Him in preparation for His ministry. After the completion of such a great task, we have no record of John feeling fearful or intimated. In fact, he declared at a point that he had to decrease while Christ's ministry would gain prominence.

When John the disciple mentioned to Jesus that they witnessed an exorcism conducted in His name and how they stopped the individual because he wasn't one of them, we see Jesus affirming that such a person shouldn't be hindered as long as he wasn't an opposition to the true Gospel.

Godly leaders are not insecure; they are not intimidated by the rise of other leaders. In fact, they support such rising leaders to ensure they fulfil their potential. Unfortunately, we see leaders trying to dim the light of others in a bid to sustain relevance. This will always backfire! The earlier we realize that better, wealthier, wiser, etc. people will emerge, and we play our part in their ascension, the better for us.

- ◈ 70 -

SUBORDINATES JOSTLING

"But to sit at my right or left is not for me to grant.
These places belong to those for whom they have been
prepared. When the ten heard about this, they became
indignant with James and John."
Mark 10:40, 41, NIV

We spoke of this briefly in the analysis regarding the hard cup the disciples would drink. In the book of Mark, another scenario that played out must be considered by leaders: when subordinates jostle for stuff.

Whether a leader is conscious of it or not, those who surround the throne always want to be the most favoured, the most considered and the most rewarded. A godly leader must, therefore, do everything within his power to handle such a situation with wisdom. This is because nothing tears apart the fabric of a leader's circle than when self-interest is the order of the day.

When a leader has more people who seek to gratify their own desires than those who seek the common good, the general populace will hardly get the very best of the vision of such a leader. Hence, godly leaders must nip in the bud any appearance of such a spirit, even addressing the same in the open if need be (as in the case of Jesus). This is one

of those hard conversations leaders must have to eliminate the "I" stance and reinforce the "we" culture.

- ⬧71 -

UNPOPULAR DECISIONS

"On reaching Jerusalem, Jesus entered the
temple courts and began driving out those who were
buying and selling there. He overturned the tables of
the money changers and the benches of those selling doves,
and would not allow anyone to carry merchandise through
the temple courts. And as he taught them, he said, 'Is it not
written: My house will be called a house of prayer
for all nations'? But you have made it
'a den of robbers.'"
Mark 11:15, 16, NIV

As a leader, if you think you will always appear good in the eyes of others, I would rather you tended to a garden. With leadership, there are some hard and very unpopular decisions that you may find yourself making.

They may not endear you to the majority, at least in the near term, and may bring widespread condemnation and disapproval. As long as such decisions are godly, fair, just and appropriate for the season, you shouldn't be discouraged from executing them. Considering the portion of Scripture above, imagine how really offensive Jesus' unpopular decision would be to those individuals hindering people from experiencing true worship in the temple!

To interpret this in the modern day, Jesus was unafraid of what the press would report the following day or the displeasure that would subsequently greet His decision on social media. The gem here is that leaders should learn to make unpopular decisions that are righteous and timely without fear or favour. Afterwards, refrain from trying so hard to prove a point to anyone. Leave the rest to God who will vindicate you.

THE BOOK OF
LUKE

– ◇ 72 –

KEEP YOUR OWN ACCOUNT

*"Many have undertaken to draw up an account
of the things that have been fulfilled among us, just as
they were handed down to us by those who from the first
were eyewitnesses and servants of the word. With this
in mind, since I myself have carefully investigated everything
from the beginning, I too decided to write an orderly
account for you, most excellent Theophilus..."*
Luke 1:1-3, NIV

Account keeping is absolutely vital. I am a strong advocate of the same, and I have, over the years, advised many leaders on keeping good records and penning down their experiences. We see Dr Luke, one of the authors of the Gospels and author of Acts, revealing the importance of keeping accounts. He wrote an orderly account after conducting a careful investigation.

A leader's role does not exempt him from keeping an orderly account of his stewardship. Truth be told, time and posterity have been unkind to those who disregarded this gem. While there is nothing wrong with other people giving accounts of your deeds and attainments, you shouldn't abdicate your responsibility of doing the same so that people can "hear from the horse's mouth". There is no denying that, if you are an upright man, the account you will give of your achievements and stewardship is likely to be more accurate than what others will testify of you.

- ◇ 73 -

TRAIN THE LITTLE ONES
TO START EARLY

*"After three days they found him in the temple courts,
sitting among the teachers, listening to them and
asking them questions. Everyone who heard him was
amazed at his understanding and his answers."*
Luke 2:47, NIV

Jesus, at a young age, showcased when young ones should be exposed to teachings and principles to prepare them for life and destiny. The family of Joseph and Mary went to Jerusalem for the festival of the Passover when Jesus was twelve. After the festival was over, and His parents were returning home, He stayed behind without His family's consent. Thinking He was with them, they had travelled for a day before realizing He was missing. After three days, they found Him in the temple courts, sitting among the teachers, keenly listening to them and asking them questions.

His parents rebuked Him as per the anxiety He had caused them. His reply was instructive concerning where young leaders should be found. Jesus expected that His mother should know He would be at the place of learning. It, therefore, shouldn't come as a surprise that He turned out to be the Leader of leaders.

Young leaders should be empowered through exposure to constant learning. This is where the formative work is established, and godly leaders shouldn't be found wanting as regards playing their roles to achieve the same. If this is done, we will raise more future leaders who are prepared for the work ahead.

- ◇ 74 -

NEVER OUTSHINE THE MASTER

"The people were waiting expectantly and were
all wondering in their hearts if John might possibly
be the Messiah. John answered them all, 'I baptize you
with water. But one who is more powerful than I will come,
the straps of whose sandals I am not worthy to untie.
He will baptize you with the Holy Spirit and fire.'"
Luke 3:15, 16, NIV

Your being a leader shouldn't excuse the possibility of you having superiors. For this reason, you must be wise enough not to attempt to outshine your master.

Jesus described John the Baptizer as the greatest of all prophets and deservedly so. Before the emergence of Jesus' ministry, John oversaw a ministry that reconciled people to the Father. Although he baptized with water, he admitted that someone with a greater measure of baptism would later emerge. John acknowledged that he was unworthy of untying the straps of Jesus' sandals because he knew full well that Jesus was God, his Creator, taking a fleshly form! Do not fall for the devil's snare of believing that you are better than your superiors. The gem here is that godly leaders must remain in the place of humility and constantly deflect honour to whom it is due. As a moon, don't claim to own the light that rightly belongs to the sun!

- ◇ 75 -

WHAT IS WRITTEN OF YOU

"And the scroll of the prophet Isaiah was handed to him. Unrolling it, he found the place where it is written: 'The Spirit of the Lord is on me, because he has anointed me to proclaim good news to the poor. He has sent me to proclaim freedom for the prisoners and recovery of sight for the blind, to set the oppressed free, to proclaim the year of the Lord's favor.' Then he rolled up the scroll, gave it back to the attendant and sat down. The eyes of everyone in the synagogue were fastened on him. He began by saying to them, 'Today this scripture is fulfilled in your hearing.'"
Luke 4:17-21, NIV

There are divine declarations written of every leader, and their discovery makes the difference. It is every leader's responsibility to unveil what God has declared about them in Scripture. Jesus demonstrated exactly this in the aforesaid portion of Scripture.

Every godly leader has a place of assignment with specific instructions, and the revelation of such directives is possible only by the help of the Holy Spirit. This reality is attainable because the Bible is not just a compendium of historical accounts, but is actually a living thing. The Word is Christ Himself! As such, it contains the answers to your longstanding questions and will afford you the direction to navigate life and fulfil purpose.

History won't be kind to you if you make light of discovering what is written of you. May the Lord empower you to do justice to this.

- ◈ 76 -

DON'T BE BLIND

"He also told them this parable: 'Can the blind
lead the blind? Will they not both fall into a pit?
The student is not above the teacher, but everyone who
is fully trained will be like their teacher.'"
Luke 6:39, 40, NIV

A leader cannot afford to be blind, otherwise the result will be disastrous. Beyond physical eyes, a godly leader must possess spiritual eyes, divine insight, in order to lead others aright. Like Jesus has mentioned, the blind leading the blind can be interpreted as an ignorant man leading other ignorant people.

While physical blindness comes with its own limitations, spiritual blindness is even worse. Spiritual insight affords you the ability to see ahead of others and be proactive instead of being reactive.

Lack of divine insight is proof of a disconnect from God, the Source of all visions and wisdom. When a leader lacks such insight, they will deny their followers of the much-needed knowledge to flourish and become leaders in their own right. Any attempt to lead as a blind leader will guarantee that you and others end in a ditch of regrets and pain.

- ◇ 77 -

RULE MAKING

"Jesus replied, 'And you experts in the law, woe to you,
because you load people down with burdens they can
hardly carry, and you yourselves will not lift
one finger to help them.'"
Luke 11:46, NIV

Jesus was well known for striking the consciences of the leaders of the day. He didn't hesitate to disapprove of the burden the Pharisees placed on others with the rules they made. They overwhelmed people with burdens they couldn't help them with. Even today, varying rules and regulations which facilitate torment—rather that bring

108

ease—have been enforced in different organizations.

As godly leaders, our rules must never be interpreted as a burden that causes men to despise us and rain curses on us. Don't be the reason people experience agony and bitterness on a daily basis. Don't be the reason people needlessly treat you with contempt.

- ◈ 78 -

PRIVATE WORDS

"What you have said in the dark will be heard
in the daylight, and what you have whispered in the ear in
the inner rooms will be proclaimed from the roofs."
Luke 12:3, NIV

This is another timely reminder that leaders should be conscious of their private words and writings. Anything that should not be found in public circles shouldn't be uttered or written in the first place. In the aforementioned portion of Scripture, Jesus spoke about private utterances becoming public knowledge.

A godly leader must, therefore, be extremely wary of their conduct in the secret where their defences are often lowered. You don't want your vulnerable moments to be the reason critics and adversaries will exploit your utterances and writings. As such, you are to pay close attention to the products of your mouth and hands so that your stance won't be misconstrued, and your labour for years won't be reduced to rubble.

- ◇ 79 -

ABUNDANCE OF POSSESSIONS

"Then he said to them, 'Watch out! Be on your guard against all kinds of greed; life does not consist in an abundance of possessions.'"
Luke 12:15, NIV

Leaders must constantly be on the lookout. When we reference a watchman, we are speaking of someone who guards a space, especially at night or during vulnerable hours. Keeping this in mind helps us to clearly understand God's instruction for us (godly leaders) here. Jesus did not mince His words in admonishing us to beware of all kinds of greed which is an intense and selfish desire for something. In tying it all up, He declared that life does not consist in an abundance of possessions which a lot of leaders ignorantly and unfortunately build their entire leadership on.

While there is no arguing that God blesses His people, including leaders, materially and financially, the acquisition of earthly possessions should never be the focus of any leader. There hasn't been a single soul with such a motive that lived a fulfilled life. After death, whatever has been acquired will be inherited, enjoyed and maximized by others. We must never cease to walk in this important consciousness.

- ◈ 80 -

ALL SHALL BE ADDED

"But seek his kingdom, and these things
will be given to you as well."
Luke 12:31, NIV

Leaders seek different things which influence our motives and dealings with men and institutions. King Solomon, who sought wisdom to lead God's people, not riches or the end of his enemies, is a classic example that comes to mind.

The portion of Scripture above reveals Jesus speaking to godly leaders to subject themselves to some much-needed introspection. We ought to re-evaluate what our hearts' desires truly are. As such, He advocates that we seek first the Kingdom of God, and whatever we desire that is in line with God's pleasure will be given to us as well. Leaders must understand that God seeks purity and righteousness in the hearts of men. He delights in only individuals that seek only the interest of His Kingdom.

Unfortunately, many leaders have turned this formula on its head: they seek things first before the Kingdom. One of the major advantages of following the correct formula is that enjoying a thriving relationship with God, first, will empower us to maximize whatever the Lord gives us without taking our eyes from Him as the Author and Finisher of our faith. A leader who seeks to fulfil the number of his days to please God must seek the Kingdom first. There are no two ways about it.

- ◊ 81 -

TRAIN THE LITTLE ONES TO START EARLY

"But the one who does not know and does things
deserving punishment will be beaten with few blows.
From everyone who has been given much, much will
be demanded; and from the one who has been entrusted
with much, much more will be asked."
Luke 12:48, NIV

Leadership is quite demanding in the sense that to whom much is given, much is expected. It is a never-ending cycle that a godly leader must be prepared for. The basis for God giving you more is tied predominantly to your performance in the last responsibility.

A leader who is constantly entrusted with calls to higher responsibilities must spiritually, physically, mentally and emotionally be prepared. And he shouldn't be worried because God will not demand of anybody what He has not first empowered them to execute.

- ◈ 82 -

DECORUM IN PUBLIC PLACES

*"When someone invites you to a wedding feast,
do not take the place of honor, for a person more
distinguished than you may have been invited. If so,
the host who invited both of you will come and say to you,
'Give this person your seat.' Then, humiliated, you will have
to take the least important place. But when you are invited,
take the lowest place, so that when your host comes, he will
say to you, 'Friend, move up to a better place.' Then you
will be honored in the presence of all the other guests.
For all those who exalt themselves will be humbled, a
nd those who humble themselves will be exalted."*
Luke 14:8-11, NIV

There is an expectation of public decorum that leaders, especially godly leaders, must display. Decorum is defined as proper and polite behaviour in society. Jesus speaks of an invitation to a wedding feast and exercising restraint from hurriedly taking a place of honour. It is a lot better to be humble and yet be raised up by others to a place of honour, than to be downgraded.

In all our public dealings, we must dress, speak and generally conduct ourselves appropriately. Godly leaders must view themselves as mouthpieces of God and understand that we cannot afford to misrepresent God because people are looking up to us and emulating us. The unforgiving world will be quick to crucify godly leaders and remind them of the faith they profess if they fall short of expectations—of God's high standards.

We must never be used as examples to shame the faith that was paid for by a huge price. Therefore, the gem in this principle is that decorum must reflect in our disposition towards others.

- ◈ 83 -

PROJECT FINANCING

"Suppose one of you wants to build a tower.
Won't you first sit down and estimate the cost to see
if you have enough money to complete it? For if you lay
the foundation and are not able to finish it, everyone
who sees it will ridicule you."
Luke 14:29, NIV

There is a likelihood that your sphere of leading may involve project conception and execution. While the nature of the projects may significantly differ in size, cost and all other metrics, one common denominator is that almost all projects require a level of resources to bring them to fruition.

Jesus, while speaking to His leaders, expressed the importance of adequate planning when it comes to project financing. To interpret this leadership-wise, He emphasized that leaders are expected to first sit down with their teams and estimate the costs of projects to ascertain if there are adequate resources to complete them.

Unfortunately, many leaders fail this test and go on to lay the groundwork for a project they will never finish, thereby attracting ridicule. The importance of putting all key factors into consideration before embarking on anything cannot be overemphasized. The gem here is to ensure that adequate financing or resources must be allocated to relevant projects.

- ◇ 84 -

OCCUPY TILL I COME

*"So he called ten of his servants, and gave them ten minas
[one apiece, each equal to about a hundred days' wages] and
said to them, 'Do business [with this] until I return.'"*
Luke 19:13, AMP

In His preferred style of communicating through parables, Jesus speaks about a man of noble birth who went to a distant country to have himself appointed king and then return to base. He called ten of his servants and gave them ten minas, instructing them to do business with the same until he returned.

Jesus didn't just leave the earth after His resurrection. With the presence of the Holy Spirit in godly leaders, He has empowered them to do business—to fulfil different purposes—until His Second Coming.

Godly leaders are, therefore, not meant to cross their hands and stare blankly at the sky. We are not to isolate ourselves from the world's system we find ourselves in but rather engage it in a manner that pleases the Master—that His will be done on earth as it has been established in heaven.

THE BOOK OF
JOHN

- ✧ 85 -

LEADERS MAKE
THEMSELVES AVAILABLE

*"Now there was a Pharisee, a man named Nicodemus
who was a member of the Jewish ruling council. He came
to Jesus at night and said, 'Rabbi, we know that you are a teacher
who has come from God. For no one could perform the signs
you are doing if God were not with him.'"*
John 3:1, 2, NIV

The availability of a leader stands them out and endears them to forward-looking people. In His interaction with Nicodemus, Jesus demonstrated the importance of availability and accessibility even at night when people should be asleep or relax after the day's work. The exchange was so significant because it would be the first time that Jesus disclosed the importance of being born again to enjoy eternal life.

Also notable is the fact that Jesus made Himself available despite His tasking ministry. Of course, making yourself available should be done with wisdom. Some leaders suffer physical, mental and emotional fatigue because they think people should be able to access them at all times.

This highlights the importance of delegation of authority so that leaders can focus on other pressing matters. A case in point is the advice Moses' father-in-law Jethro gave Moses in Exodus 18. Make yourself available to people only when the occasion truly demands so.

- ◈ 86 -

LEADERS DON'T DISCRIMINATE

*"When a Samaritan woman came to draw water,
Jesus said to her, 'Will you give me a drink?' (His disciples
had gone into the town to buy food.) The Samaritan woman
said to him, 'You are a Jew, and I am a Samaritan woman.
How can you ask me for a drink?' (For Jews do not
associate with Samaritans.)"*
John 4:8-9, NIV

*"Then Jesus declared, 'I, the one
speaking to you—I am He.'"*
John 4:26, NIV

Leaders must never discriminate against others. God may gift you followers from all walks of life, so you must be careful not to deal with people based on stereotypes or preconceived notions. Leaders who discriminate against people on whatever basis make a mockery of the real concept of servant leadership which is to serve all and sundry.

While Jesus was interacting with the Samaritan woman, she didn't hesitate to bring His attention to the fact that people from both nationalities shouldn't be found together. This didn't deter Jesus because He wasn't discriminatory.

Eventually, He revealed private details of the woman's life to her, spurring her to tell people to come and behold Christ. It was in this same encounter that Jesus affirmed the real posture of worship—worshipping God in spirit and in truth. He revealed His divinity—that He had come to die for the entire human race—by showing no discrimination. Godly leaders emulate Christ. They don't erect barriers between them and those they have been called to lead.

- ◈ 87 -

LIKE GOD, LEADERS MUST KEEP WORKING

*"So, because Jesus was doing these things
on the Sabbath, the Jewish leaders began to persecute him.
In his defense Jesus said to them, 'My Father is always at his
work to this very day, and I too am working.'"*
John 5:17, NIV

Leaders keep working because hard work is a cardinal part of a leader's daily itinerary. You cannot separate a successful leader from a hardworking one. In other words, godly leaders must never be identified as lazy or indifferent to work. Jesus Christ understood that He had limited time to fulfil His purpose on earth and would spare no day—not even the Sabbath, as seen in Scripture above—to achieve the same.

Beyond your Heavenly Father and the Son receiving praises from the beings in Heaven, they are hard at work. Consequently, you, as their representative, have no excuse—not after you have been gifted all that pertains to life and Godliness.

- ◈ 88 -

AVOID GLORY HUNTING

"I do not accept glory from human beings."
John 5:41, NIV

Here, Jesus highlights a vital element of His life, which leaders must do well to adopt for their benefit: not accepting glory from human beings. In fact, God has personally instructed me to avoid seeking praise, glory and validation from men.

While there is nothing wrong with people who genuinely want to show their love and appreciation for you, God will pay close attention to your heart's posture during such moments. If we so depend on the praise and approval of people for relevance, instead of delighting ourselves in our identity in Christ, our spiritual lives will take a hit.

To sustain our effectiveness and relevance, godly leaders must never act like worldly leaders who go about seeking glory. Here, I must confess that this battle is not won overnight; we must learn to conquer it on a daily basis.

- ◈ 89 -

PREMATURE ASSERTION TO AUTHORITY

"After the people saw the sign Jesus performed,
they began to say, 'Surely this is the Prophet who is to
come into the world.' Jesus, knowing that they intended to
come and make him king by force, withdrew again
to a mountain by himself."
John 6:15, NIV

There is no arguing that you have been ordained to lead. Even people around you can discern the same. All of this can prompt you to assert yourself, but herein lies the danger: you may end up appearing on the scene prematurely. Imagine what would have happened if Jesus had come before John! According to divine orchestration, a forerunner had to introduce Him to the world and baptize Him.

This is proof that the emergence of any leader must conform to God's exact timing; premature manifestation has consequences. It can cause a man to mismanage his life, other people, resources and institutions. When Jesus knew people's intent to crown Him king was faulty, He avoided premature assertion by withdrawing from them.

Godly leaders must do everything to ensure that any announcement or appearance must be in sync with God's timing. Merely following the emotions and words of men can lead to ruin, making you and other people question your calling.

- ◈ 90 -

YOU WILL BE DESERTED

*"On hearing it, many of his disciples said,
'This is a hard teaching. Who can accept it?' Aware that
his disciples were grumbling about this, Jesus said to them,
'Does this offend you?' From this time many of his disciples
turned back and no longer followed him."*
John 6:60, 61, NIV

In the light of Jesus' deep and hard teaching about Him being the bread of life and yielding Himself so that people can have eternal life, He sensed the disciples' grumbling and enquired if His ministration offended them. Afterwards, many disciples ceased to follow Him. There was a massive dent to Jesus' following because He preached what appeared controversial.

Godly leaders must never forget that making the right call won't always win you everyone's loyalty. What is really important is implementing the right decision and identifying the core of your team who will remain and stay committed to the cause, as Peter and others did in the case of Jesus.

- ◈ 91 -

LEADERS DON'T FOLLOW THE MOB

"Jesus straightened up and asked her,
'Woman, where are they? Has no one condemned you?'
'No one, sir,' she said. 'Then neither do I condemn you,'
Jesus declared. 'Go now and leave your life of sin.'"
John 8:11, NIV

Leaders must be very intentional about not embodying the mob mentality. When the woman caught in adultery was brought to Jesus, He wasn't quick to speak or act as the mob did. He would eventually do so under the inspiration of the Holy Spirit by asking whoever was without sin to cast the first stone on her.

Upon His declaration, people exited the scene until only Jesus and the woman were left. Then, Jesus admonished her to go and sin no more. Godly leaders must take their cue from Jesus and never be cowed by mobs. They must exercise the calm and wisdom needed to judge situations correctly in the heat of the moment.

- ◈ 92 -

THE VOICE OF LEADERSHIP

*"The gatekeeper opens the gate for him, and the
sheep listen to his voice. He calls his own sheep by name
and leads them out. When he has brought out all his own,
he goes on ahead of them, and his sheep follow him
because they know his voice."*
John 10:3, 4, NIV

Leadership has a distinct voice that godly leaders must be conscious of. Just like the case of the sheep that listened to and obeyed the master's voice, according to Scripture above, followers will listen to and obey leaders that they have learnt to trust over time. This is achieved through a close, active relationship that is nurtured with wisdom and purposefulness.

To build a voice of leadership, godly leaders must spend quality time with their followers. They must familiarize themselves with their followers' identities, strengths, shortcomings, aspirations and so on. In due time, trust and loyalty will be established, and such a leader-follower relationship will experience greater clarity going forward.

- ◈ 93 -

BRINGING ALL UNDER
YOUR LEADERSHIP

"I have other sheep that are not of this sheep pen.
I must bring them also. They too will listen to my voice,
and there shall be one flock and one shepherd."
John 10:16, NIV

Upon studying leaders who have overseen various jurisdictions, multicultural societies or global organizations, I can affirm that the only true possibility of recording any form of success is by bringing all under your leadership.

Like Jesus' mission to bring all sheep into His fold, a godly leader must be able to bring all stakeholders under the "roof" of what he seeks to achieve. The inability to do so will see a rising of splinter leaders across the board, who will instigate disunity and cause your leadership to be faced with opposition and disloyalty. May the Lord give you the required wisdom and resolve to navigate this course correctly.

- ◈ 94 -

EMPATHY

"Jesus wept."
John 11:35, NIV

Jesus experienced humanity and divinity while on earth. As a Human, He didn't fail to showcase one defining quality of godly leaders: empathy. Empathy is defined as the ability to sense other people's emotions, coupled with the ability to imagine what someone else might be thinking or feeling.

In the narrative of Lazarus' death, we can see how Jesus demonstrated empathy by weeping along with the deceased's loved ones. Doing that proved the humanity aspect of Him could really relate to the feelings of man.

Godly leaders who fail to be empathetic will lack any meaningful connection with those they lead. Beyond the rational, it is important to connect with people emotionally. This shows people that you really care and are not merely using them to achieve an end.

It, therefore, doesn't come as a surprise that Scripture admonishes us to rejoice with those who rejoice and mourn with the bereaved. Never be found wanting as regards putting your emotions to good use.

THE BOOK OF
ACTS

- ◈ 95 -

NO GAP IN LEADERSHIP

"'For,' said Peter, 'it is written in the Book of Psalms:
'May his place be deserted; let there be no one to dwell in it,'
and, 'May another take his place of leadership.'"
Acts 1:20, NIV

Leadership abhors a vacuum in any form. After Judas had committed suicide in the wake of betraying Jesus for thirty pieces of silver, the twelve disciples became eleven, and the vacuum needed to be occupied. Later, Jesus would ascend to heaven, and the Holy Spirit took His place, empowering the disciples to do the work of ministry.

In a bid to replace the deceased Judas, lots were cast on Barsabas and Matthias after praying. The lot fell on Matthias, and the void was filled. Godly leaders must appreciate how God is intentional about ensuring no vacuum is left unattended. Therefore, we must do the same, ensuring that all crucial positions are filled so that our leadership is thoroughly maximized.

- 💎 96 -

HONOUR GIVES YOU A VOICE

"But a Pharisee named Gamaliel, a teacher of the law,
who was honored by all the people, stood up in the Sanhedrin
and ordered that the men be put outside for a little while.
Then he addressed the Sanhedrin: 'Men of Israel,
consider carefully what you intend to do to these men.'"
Acts 5:34, 35, NIV

A leader in the circle of other leaders must command honour; this prompts people to grant him listening ears. Many are just leaders by title; they lack a voice that is respected and obeyed.

According to the Biblical text above, the Apostles were emboldened by the Holy Spirit and had become a menace to the religious establishment who had assumed that the killing of their Leader, Jesus, would spell the end of Christianity. During an encounter, Peter declared that the Apostles would rather obey God than men.

The men were furious and plotted to kill them, but a Pharisee by the name of Gamaliel, a teacher of the law who was greatly honoured by all the people addressed those present. He took them on a history ride of how movements not sponsored by God naturally died off. Further, he advised that the Apostles should be left alone because if their deeds were of the flesh, they would perish eventually. They all agreed with him because he commanded honour.

In every gathering, godly leaders must embody an honourable voice that other leaders respect, acknowledge and follow. We must never play second fiddle to the fleshly views of others, knowing that we carry the wisdom of God.

- ◈ 97 -

RESPONSIBILITIES – THE SPIRIT AND WISDOM

"Brothers and sisters, choose seven men from among
you who are known to be full of the Spirit and wisdom.
We will turn this responsibility over to them."
Acts 6:3, NIV

The early church was growing fast; with this exponential growth naturally came disagreements. In particular, there was a complaint against the Hebrews by the Hellenists because the latter's widows were neglected in the daily distribution of food. In effect, the Apostles decided to choose deacons who would manage kitchen affairs while they focused on the ministry of prayer and the Word.

The criterion for selecting the deacons was that they must be full of the Holy Spirit and wisdom. While job descriptions demand certain skills and parameters for engagement, I strongly believe that a godly leader should keep a lookout for the presence of the Spirit of God and wisdom in the lives of those he has decided to entrust roles to. Your possessing these qualities, to begin with, makes verifying them in other people an easy task.

- ♦ 98 -

STICK TO CORE FUNCTIONS

*"And we will give our attention to prayer
and the ministry of the word."*
Acts 6:4, NIV

Godly and purposeful leaders understand the necessity of sticking to their core functions. As such, it is absolutely vital that leaders create a distinction between areas where they function best and areas where they are passive.

While the Apostles understood the importance of having food distributed without favouritism, they wouldn't neglect the weightier matter of pressing deeper into God to know His will for the early church, through the dual ministry of prayer and the Word. As such, they delegated food management to other leaders—the deacons.

Godly leaders must never be inclined towards majoring on the minor and minoring on the major. We are to emulate

134

the commendable resolve of the Apostles to maintain laser focus on what really matters.

- ◈ 99 -

THE BEST TALENT CAN BE IN THE KITCHEN

"Now Stephen, a man full of God's grace and power, performed great wonders and signs among the people."
Acts 6:8, NIV

I have often believed that sometimes the best talents can be found in the unlikeliest of places. We may readily conclude that those in the spotlight or under constant public scrutiny may be God's favourites. No doubt, they hold a special place, but God, whose ways are not man's ways, sometimes leaves His prized jewels like Stephen in relatively lowly places. Stephen so demonstrated the power and wisdom of God that members of the Synagogue of the Freedmen conspired against him, secretly persuading some men to accuse him of blasphemy.

Stephen would later stand before the Sanhedrin with a face like that of an angel. He gave a speech that would be a reference for all generations, chronicling the genesis of our faith walk and how unrepentant the people were. This led to his stoning after he became the first person in Bible records to see Jesus standing at the right hand of God—after His ascension. This is quite impressive for a man entrusted with food management. Godly leaders must stay discerning and feel the pulse of the talents around them; your best talent may be in the kitchen.

- ◈ 100 -

SPEECH AND ACTION

*"Moses was educated in all the wisdom of
the Egyptians and was powerful in speech and action."*
Acts 7:22, NIV

Leaders struggle with what is expected of them, especially when they are lacking in the area of education and training. There is a place for formal education and also the education of life. Any leader possessing both will manifest unique wisdom and become powerful not just in speech but also in action.

When Stephen spoke about the faith walk of the Israelites to highlight how they had departed from God, he referenced how well educated Moses was in all the wisdom of the Egyptians. This could easily have been ignored, but we must understand that Moses' knowledge of the enemy eventually became a major advantage in his leadership journey.

For a godly leader to command power in speech and decision-making, he mustn't treat all forms of relevant education, including formal education and experiential knowledge, with scant regard.

- ◈ 101 -

THE WRONG CONVICTION

"Meanwhile, Saul was still breathing out murderous
threats against the Lord's disciples. He went to the
high priest and asked him for letters to the synagogues
in Damascus, so that if he found any there who belonged
to the Way, whether men or women, he might take
them as prisoners to Jerusalem."
Acts 9:2, NIV

A leader can pursue a wrong cause that can be driven by a faulty source of conviction. After Stephen had delivered his speech, he was dragged out by the yelling mob, and they began to stone him. Meanwhile, the false witnesses laid out their coats at the feet of a young man named Saul who the Bible says approved of his killing.

The era of church persecution was spearheaded by Saul who was pursuing a wrong cause from a place of perceived right doing. He started to destroy the church by going from house to house, dragging off both men and women and putting them in prison. This Pharisee and lawyer who understood the Mosaic law thought the Lord was pleased with his misguided zeal and actions. Not only that, he got letters of approval to persecute Christians in Damascus.

On his journey, he graciously encountered Jesus and ended up realizing that he was pursuing a wrong cause. He would eventually become Apostle Paul, one of the most influential figures of the New Testament, who wrote the Epistles that even modern-day believers hold so dearly.

Godly leaders must remain conscious so as not to tread the path of Saul. Misguided actions, which are anchored to faulty convictions, serve no righteous purpose.

- ◈ 102 -

LEARN TO ASCRIBE PRAISE TO GOD ALONE

*"On the appointed day Herod, wearing his
royal robes, sat on his throne and delivered a public address
to the people. They shouted, 'This is the voice of a god,
not of a man.' Immediately, because Herod did not give
praise to God, an angel of the Lord struck him down,
and he was eaten by worms and died."*
Acts 12:21-23, NIV

The wisdom in deflecting praise is something I have seen a lot of influential and wise leaders exhibit; they use a combination of tact and humility to ensure that the praise of men does not fully envelop them, causing them to fall. Herod had gone from Judea to Caesarea due to his quarrel with the people of Tyre and Sidon. The parties later got an intermediary close to the king, seeking peace because of their dependence on Herod's country for food.

On the appointed day of the meeting, the king appeared in his royal robe and delivered what must have been a glowing speech. Consequently, his subjects declared that his voice was that of a god and not a man. Immediately those words sank into his eardrums, he soaked in the adulation and failed to give praise to God. Thereafter, an angel struck him, and he died after being consumed by worms.

Godly leaders must learn that God will never share His praise with any mortal being. As such, you must be wise enough to handle the praise of men. Your default heart's posture must be ascribing all the glory and praise to your Maker and never equating yourself with Him. King Nebuchadnezzer also failed in this regard, and he reaped the consequences.

- ◈ 103 -

BE WARY OF MISLEADING ADVISERS

*"They traveled through the whole island until
they came to Paphos. There they met a Jewish sorcerer
and false prophet named Bar-Jesus, who was an attendant
of the proconsul, Sergius Paulus. The proconsul,
an intelligent man, sent for Barnabas and Saul because he
wanted to hear the word of God. But Elymas the sorcerer
(for that is what his name means) opposed them and tried
to turn the proconsul from the faith."*
Acts 13:7, 8, NIV

Some leaders' greatest undoing is that they have surrounded themselves with ungodly advisers, as in the case of Sergius Paulus and the sorcerer Bar-Jesus. Sergio Paulus was the Proconsul of the Island of Paphos who, despite his intelligence, had a spiritual attendant and false prophet by the name of Bar-Jesus.

Due to Sergius' hunger for knowledge, he sent for Barnabas and Saul to hear the Word of God. However, Bar-Jesus (or Elymas) opposed them and tried to turn the proconsul from the faith. Paul's rebuke led to Elymas' blindness and the strengthening of Sergius' belief in the Gospel.

One can only wonder how many years the proconsul had received what could have been devilish advice from the sorcerer despite the proconsul's acknowledged intelligence. Godly leaders must realize that their intelligence will be of little or no effect if they are surrounded by their own version of Bar-Jesus. The outcome is never palatable, so leaders must steer clear of such people.

- ◈ 104 -

PREPARE YOUR LIEUTENANTS FROM INEVITABLE HOSTILITY

"Paul wanted to take him along on the journey,
so he circumcised him because of the Jews who lived in
that area, for they all knew that his father was a Greek."
Acts 16:3, NIV

Leaders are constantly rising up to the challenge of preparing those they take to battle. They understand that there will be inevitable hostility, and when they can't be touched, the opposition will confront those closest to them.

Timothy, who joined Paul and Silas, had a good report. Paul wanted to take him along, but because his mother was Jewish and his father was Greek, he knew he would face great hostility from the Jews in their destination. For that reason, Paul subjected him to circumcision, effectively eliminating what could have been a hindrance to the acceptance of the Gospel.

Godly leaders, like Paul, mustn't await the emergence of

potential problems before tackling them. Beyond you, ensure your lieutenants are also well prepared for the journey ahead.

- ◈ 105 -

SCRUTINY

"Now the Berean Jews were of more noble character than those in Thessalonica, for they received the message with great eagerness and examined the Scriptures every day to see if what Paul said was true."
Acts 17:11, NIV

One of the reasons godly leaders must be thoroughly equipped to deliver on their responsibilities is that they shouldn't merely expect the led to swallow everything they say hook, line and sinker. Any leader that detests being subjected to scrutiny from time to time might as well bid leadership farewell.

In Scripture above, we can see how the Berean Christians subjected Paul's ministry to scrutiny. They wouldn't be swayed by his name and accomplishments and had to ascertain that his teachings were thoroughly consistent with God's Word.

Godly leaders must never be complacent because they will certainly encounter people who will test their leadership credibility, not necessarily out of pessimism or hatred, but to ensure they are not being misled. You cannot afford to disappoint God and man, so be equal to the task handed to you.

- ◈ 106 -

EARNING A LIVING

"And because he was a tentmaker as they were,
he stayed and worked with them."
Acts 18:3, NIV

This verse reveals the hardworking and entrepreneurial nature of Paul. By contrast, many modern leaders would rather be fed by their followers and become a leech on them. Having left Athens, Paul went to Corinth and met Aquila and Priscilla there. Scripture testifies that he was a tentmaker as they were, and he stayed and worked with them.

One way by which a leader demonstrates exemplary leadership is that he works to earn a living. Doing so brought dignity on Paul as no one could lay claim to him taking advantage of anyone financially. Godly leaders must imbibe this quality so as to earn the respect of the led who should ensure that leaders' conduct conforms to godly standards before they emulate it.

- 💎 107 -

ENCOURAGING LEADERS AND CONVERTS

*"After spending some time in Antioch,
Paul set out from there and traveled from
place to place throughout the region of Galatia
and Phrygia, strengthening all the disciples."*
Acts 18:23, NIV

The book of Acts chronicles the activities of the leaders of the early church, including those geared towards encouraging the leaders and converts of those churches, as well as converts established in other regions. Therefore, the Apostles and leaders such as Paul had the mandate to constantly encourage other leaders and those who were new to the faith.

Similarly, godly leaders must ensure they encourage those who are answerable to them. They have a calling to reach out far and wide and constantly inspire the new generation of leaders who must execute the vision and carry on with the work. Back in the day, Paul used feathers to create writings on papyrus. Now, with modern technology, leaders have no excuse not to leverage all available resources to fully equip the forthcoming generation.

– ♦ 108 –

BE READY FOR DEBATES

"When Apollos wanted to go to Achaia,
the brothers and sisters encouraged him
and wrote to the disciples there to welcome him.
When he arrived, he was a great help to those
who by grace had believed. For he vigorously
refuted his Jewish opponents in public debate,
proving from the Scriptures that
Jesus was the Messiah."
Acts 18:28, NIV

"Paul entered the synagogue
and spoke boldly there for three months,
arguing persuasively about the kingdom of God."
Acts 19:8, NIV

"But some of them became obstinate;
they refused to believe and publicly maligned the Way.
So Paul left them. He took the disciples with him
and had discussions daily in the
lecture hall of Tyrannus."
Acts 19:9, NIV

There is something I particularly like about the parliamentary system of government, which is the fact that leaders of the political units must be ready for debates on policies and pressing national issues. Debates birth robust mental stimulation and solutions that passive conversations may not be able to achieve. Leaders should embody this mindset so that they won't be caught unawares when they are put on the spot.

In the time of Paul, we see how Apollos, after being taught the way of God more adequately by Priscilla and Aquila, refuted his Jewish opponents in a public debate to prove from the Scriptures that Jesus was the Messiah. Also, we see Paul himself entering the synagogue and speaking boldly there for three months; he argued persuasively about the Kingdom of God and also had discussions daily in the lecture hall of Tyrannus.

A leader must be prepared for difficult exchanges. The church, I believe, is entering into an era where many people will have to declare Jesus' lordship more than ever before so that more souls can be reconciled to God or taught the Gospel rightly. By extension, godly leaders in any sphere of influence must be ready for verbal discourses to authenticate their leadership and the messages they carry.

- ◈ 109 -

LANGUAGE IS A CONNECTOR

"When they heard him speak to them in Aramaic,
they became very quiet."
Acts 22:2, NIV

There are some languages I honestly wish I spoke. In fact, I encourage my children to learn as many languages, not just for the fun of it or because of the little advantage they may enjoy when they exercise multilingualism. I do so most especially because language is an effective connector to people. Leaders must understand that nothing breaks down barriers faster than language.

After allegations of defilement had been preferred against Apostle Paul, he showcased how powerful language is by asking if the Roman commander spoke Greek. Not only that, he introduced himself and asked that he speak to the people. After receiving permission, he spoke to them in Aramaic; and, according to the Bible, they became very quiet when they heard him.

Godly leaders must leverage the power and bond fostered by language in their engagements with the led. People will naturally gravitate towards you when they hear their local languages roll off your tongue. The resolve to learn multiple languages, local or foreign, is worth it; the dividends are immense.

- ◈ 110 -

THINK ON YOUR FEET

"Then Paul, knowing that some of them were Sadducees
and the others Pharisees, called out in the Sanhedrin,
'My brothers, I am a Pharisee, descended from Pharisees.
I stand on trial because of the hope of the resurrection of the dead.'
When he said this, a dispute broke out between the Pharisees
and the Sadducees, and the assembly was divided.
(The Sadducees say that there is no resurrection,
and that there are neither angels nor spirits,
but the Pharisees believe all these things.)"
Act 23:6-8, NIV

Any leader that will stand the test of time must possess the ability to think on their feet. This skill will empower a leader to escape from many unpleasant situations.

After his address to the mob, Paul was taken into the barracks to avoid a riot. An instruction was given that he should be flogged, but this didn't happen because he disclosed his dual nationality—he was a Roman and a Jew. In fact, the commander was stunned that he put a Roman in chains. The next day, the commander released Paul and ordered the chief priests and all the members of the Sanhedrin to assemble. The Sanhedrin, a supreme council and tribunal of the Jews during postexilic times (period before the Babylonian captivity), was headed by a high priest who exercised jurisdiction over religious, civil and criminal matters.

Paul was aware that the Sanhedrin contained both Pharisees and Sadducees who didn't have the same mindset about resurrection. At this juncture, he thought on his feet: he didn't hesitate to reveal his Pharisaic identity and affirm his belief in resurrection as other Pharisees do. This led to a dispute between both groups—of course, the Sadducees didn't believe in resurrection—and the assembly was divided.

The uproar was so much that the commander feared Paul would be torn to pieces and ordered his troops to take him away. Coincidentally—and instructively so—we see two examples of how a godly leader can exercise wisdom in tight moments. We must emulate this because we won't always be afforded ample opportunity to analyze matters.

- ◈ 111 -

A CLEAR CONSCIENCE

"So I strive always to keep my conscience
clear before God and man."
Acts 24:16, NIV

One of my favourite quotes, while growing up, was seen at the back of a popular Nigerian newspaper. It made, and still makes, an impression on my mind. It is rendered thus: "A conscience is like an open wound; only the truth can heal it." Conscience can be defined as a person's moral sense of right and wrong, a sense or consciousness of the moral goodness or blameworthiness of one's conduct or intentions. Every man has a part of them that judges their actions—that makes them feel guilty in the event of a misstep.

Paul, as a leader, advocates that all men must strive to always keep their consciences clear before God and other people, just like he did. Godly leaders must understand that only a clear conscience can give a leader the kind of right standing, the kind of voice to be respected and the audacity to take certain actions without fear or favour. Many leaders often find themselves constrained by a guilty conscience; that is, they are unable to fully express themselves because they have fallen short of their own moral sense of what is right and wrong.

Leaders who easily compromise will always have cloudy consciences before God and men. It is, therefore, imperative that we maintain a good standing always. Doing so makes heaven testify about us confidently, and we don't have to bother about any evil done in the secret that will later become public knowledge.

- ◈ 112 -

KICK AGAINST THE GOADS

"We all fell to the ground, and I heard a voice
saying to me in Aramaic, 'Saul, Saul,
why do you persecute me? It is hard for you
to kick against the goads.'"
Acts 26:14, NIV

Leaders must understand that when they conduct themselves in ungodly ways, they will hurt themselves and, by extension, others.

In ancient times, goads were typically made from slender pieces of timber, blunt at one end and pointed at the other. Farmers used the pointed end to urge a stubborn ox into motion; and, occasionally, the beast could kick at the goad which would pierce its leg and cause immense pain.

Godly leaders must avoid kicking against the goads. We must avoid being like the Saul who had yet to encounter Jesus—the headstrong Saul—who maintained a course of action (persecuting Christians) that hurt lives and families.

- ◈ 113 -

ENCOURAGEMENT
AMIDST HOPELESSNESS

*"Just before dawn Paul urged them all to eat.
'For the last fourteen days,' he said, 'you have been
in constant suspense and have gone without
food—you haven't eaten anything. Now I urge you
to take some food. You need it to survive. Not one of you
will lose a single hair from his head.' After he said this,
he took some bread and gave thanks to God in front
of them all. Then he broke it and began to eat.
They were all encouraged and ate
some food themselves."*
Acts 27:33-36, NIV

The encouragement from leaders, even amidst hopelessness, reveals the apex of leadership. During Paul's final journey to Rome to stand before Caesar, he informed his fellow travellers about his perception that the voyage would be disrupted via significant damage to the ship. Unfortunately, the centurion believed the master and owner of the ship instead of Paul.

Eventually, a great storm would emerge, causing the damage of the ship as Paul rightly declared. Thankfully, no life was lost. One can only imagine the terror that enveloped the men before, during and after the shipwreck. In fact, hopelessness so gripped everyone that none had eaten for fourteen days.

Paul wouldn't allow the despair to linger, so he got bread, thanked God for the same and began eating. This prompted others to take their cue from him. A leader is like a bright lantern in the thick darkness; he is always a beacon of hope in the midst of hopelessness. When it appears like there's nothing to hold on to, godly leaders must rise to the occasion and make the led see reasons to live for another day.

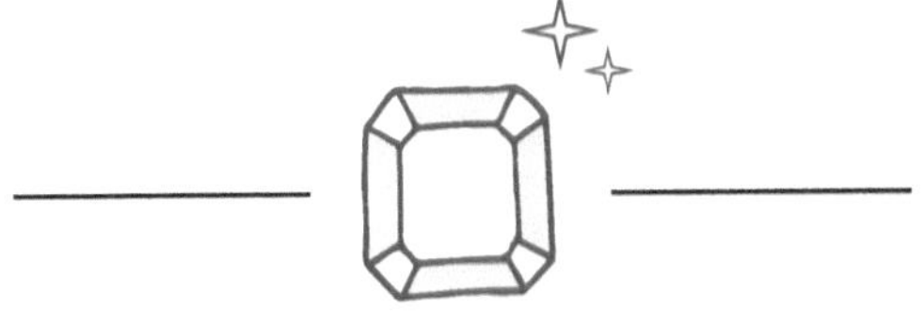

THE BOOK OF
ROMANS

- 114 -

CONSTANT INTERCESSION

*"God whom I serve in my spirit in preaching
the gospel of his Son, is my witness how constantly
I remember you in my prayers at all times; and I pray
that now at last by God's will the way may be
opened for me to come to you."*
Romans 1:9, 10, NIV

Godly leaders, after the likeness of Christ, are to operate in the dual office of priest and king. It is, therefore, a heavenly duty to take up the priestly role of interceding on behalf of your followers and your sphere of control. This was clearly demonstrated by Apostle Paul to the Roman church.

Sadly, we have a generation of leaders who have forsaken the role and importance of prayer; many have outsourced their spiritual authority to "prayer warriors" because they are "too busy" to pray. By neglecting intercession, such leaders have become victims of both physical and spiritual assaults. Worse still, some have been duped financially.

Godly leaders understand that there is a time to take on the priestly ephod to call on the God of all flesh. We see leaders in the Old Testament who engaged intercession, and it augured well for their reign and followers. Godly leaders who are underutilizing their spiritual capacity or have abandoned the same altogether must reintroduce constant and purposeful intercession to truly lead in a way that attracts peace and prosperity. The government houses, business headquarters and social clubs should become places of prayers.

- ◻ 115 -

KINDNESS AND STERNNESS

*"Consider therefore the kindness and sternness of God:
sternness to those who fell, but kindness to you,
provided that you continue in his kindness.
Otherwise, you also will be cut off."*
Romans 11:22, NIV

Leaders should consider and ponder about how God executes His leadership style. His kindness and severity are two sides of the same coin, and you will experience either attribute based on your actions.

Notably, I have often heard preachers discuss how Jesus is known as both Lion and Lamb, creatures with contrasting attributes. While the former is very fierce and dominant, the latter is extremely gentle and meek. A leader who appears to be too stern will isolate many, lack empathy and deal with issues forcefully, only to get few to no results.

On the other hand, a leader who is just a "lamb" will appear too gentle and may easily be overrun by individuals who will take his meekness for granted. Note, according to Scripture above, that God was kind to those deserving of His kindness and severe to those worthy of His sternness. Godly leaders must work with this two-pronged approach for effective leadership.

- ◻ 116 -

MIND TRANSFORMATION

"Do not conform to the pattern of this world,
but be transformed by the renewing of your mind.
Then you will be able to test and approve what
God's will is—his good, pleasing and perfect will."
Romans 12:2, NIV

There is a place for mind transformation, and I believe it makes all the difference in the quality of leadership exhibited. Exemplary leadership which is well sought after is birthed from a transformed mind.

Paul delivered a timely admonition to the Roman church that they should steer clear of adopting the mindsets and lifestyle of the world. Of course, this speaks to even modern-day leaders. Instead, godly leaders are to be transformed, which is possible only through constant mind renewal. This is achieved through exposure to, and meditation on, God's precepts as embodied by the Scriptures. It is only after the foregoing has been achieved that one can rightly discern God's will.

A godly leader who seeks to do God's will can achieve the same only when they are non-conformists who are constantly undergoing spiritual renewing. The state of the heart should never be taken for granted because the issues of life emerge from there.

- 117 -

BEWARE OF PRIDE

"For by the grace given me I say to every one of you:
Do not think of yourself more highly than you ought,
but rather think of yourself with sober judgment,
in accordance with the faith God has
distributed to each of you."
Romans 12:3, NIV

"We have different gifts, according to the grace
given to each of us. If your gift is prophesying,
then prophesy in accordance with your faith;
if it is serving, then serve; if it is teaching, then teach;
if it is to encourage, then give encouragement;
if it is giving, then give generously; if it is to lead,
do it diligently; if it is to show mercy, do it cheerfully."
Romans 12:6, 7, NIV

Paul admonishes Christians, including righteous leaders, to assess themselves soberly, based on the faith God has given them, and not tread the path of pride. Worryingly, pride is one of the major reasons leaders fail. This is corroborated by the Bible which declares that pride precedes destruction.

Pride manifests when one begins to overestimate oneself and attempts to play god in the lives of others. This is why godly leaders have been warned to evaluate themselves only through faith. For instance, a leader, through faith, understands that there is nothing he owns that wasn't first given to him from above. With such understanding, he will never look down on others who appear not to be as (multi-)talented as he is. Everyone is blessed, as determined by God, with different gifts to fulfil different purposes.

By virtue of our gifts and positions, we must refrain from thinking we are better than others, even those we lead. Leadership is, indeed, an election of grace that must cause humility to be our constant watchword.

- 118 -

LOVE IN ACTION

"Love must be sincere. Hate what is evil;
cling to what is good."
Romans 12:9, NIV

Here, Paul simply affirms that the demonstration of love must stem from sincerity. In other words, leaders are to show sincere love to others around them, knowing full well that the recipients of our disposition can sense whether or not we are genuine.

A godly leader must give sincere love to everyone, including those who are undeserving of the same in our opinion. The second half of the admonition is hatred for all evil things. A godly leader must be extremely vocal about their disdain for evil, as they tightly hold on to what is good.

- 💎 119 -

SWITCH ACCORDINGLY

"Rejoice with those who rejoice;
mourn with those who mourn."
Romans 12:15, NIV

The chameleon stands out for its ability to mirror the prevalent colour of its immediate surroundings. Similarly, Paul asserted the importance of conducting ourselves according to the prevalent mood in every situation: we are to rejoice with those who are joyful and mourn with the bereaved.

Jesus must have demonstrated this exemplary conduct at the wedding in Cana and the location of Lazarus' burial. Godly leaders must be wise enough to display the right emotions to bring the led closer to them as they journey towards achieving a common goal.

- 120 -

AVOID CURSING

"Bless those who persecute you;
bless and do not curse."
Romans 12:14, NIV

This could appear like a tall order, especially considering how painful it is for any leader to be persecuted unjustly or opposed needlessly. But we must never forget that God's commandments are not burdensome; He has made grace available to implement every of His instructions.

I have, through a particular community leadership position, found myself in this boat. It was a thankless job, yet I found myself in a needless lawsuit against a member of that community. I painfully wondered what I had done to deserve any sort of persecution, but the truth is emotional people cannot obey scriptural demands. Come what may, curses must never be found on the lips of godly leaders. Whether it is convenient or not, our default mode must always be to bless people.

- 121 -

HARMONIOUS LIVING

*"Live in harmony with one another.
Do not be proud, but be willing to associate with
people of low position. Do not be conceited."*
Romans 12:16, NIV

The world will be much better if we all live in harmony! We are expected to live in harmony and humble ourselves well enough to associate with people of low positions. Leaders often struggle with this admonition because their exalted offices have a way of establishing segregation between the common man and them. This disconnect has been among the greatest undoing of many leaders who lose touch with reality.

Godly leaders must create harmonious atmospheres around them and frown upon all manner of discrimination. Often, ascension to leadership means the relegation of those occupying lowly positions, and this must be discouraged. We should learn from the greatest Man who ever lived on earth—Jesus—who, although God, didn't hesitate to relate directly to His creations (humans) to achieve His purpose.

- ◻ 122 -

OVERCOMING EVIL WITH GOOD

"Do not repay anyone evil for evil.
Be careful to do what is right in the eyes of everyone."
Romans 12:17, NIV

The inclination towards rewarding evil with evil, I must admit, resides permanently in the hearts of many. When people are hurt by other people's utterances or actions, the next thing on their minds is vengeance. The presence of such in the heart of a leader can have disastrous consequences due to the fact that he most likely commands a wealth of human, natural, material and financial resources with which he can get revenge easily.

A godly leader must never be caught in the trap of paying people back in the same coin. While the worldly system encourages an eye for an eye, righteous leaders resolve to please God by walking in love even in the face of evil. Besides the primary purpose of representing Christ correctly, never forget that the led who look up to you will always keep a lookout for your response during unpalatable situations. You cannot afford to disappoint them as well.

- 💎 123 -

PEACE

*"If it is possible, as far as it depends on you,
live at peace with everyone."*
Romans 12:18, NIV

Living peacefully with all men may appear impossible on the surface. This is because there are many who will never be happy or satisfied with you, just like everyone won't make you happy or satisfied. Paul, therefore, admonishes that we should deal peacefully with everyone as God has granted us the capacity. Also, "as far as it depends on you" means you should act righteously regardless of the other party's disposition.

The reason many leaders often struggle with this instruction is that they are more concerned about the acts of others instead of what is within their control: their own action. Living peacefully should be the watchword of every godly leader in their dealings with people from all walks of life and people with varying flaws.

- 124 -

REVENGE

*"Do not take revenge, my dear friends,
but leave room for God's wrath, for it is written:
'It is mine to avenge; I will repay,' says the Lord.
On the contrary: 'If your enemy is hungry, feed him;
if he is thirsty, give him something to drink. In doing this,
you will heap burning coals on his head.'"*
Romans 12:19, 20, NIV

In one of the previous gems, I talked about refraining from seeking vengeance or taking revenge. As leaders, we must leave room for God's wrath if need be. Only God has the ability to execute judgement without getting corrupted. You can rest assured that seeking revenge on your own terms will ultimately corrupt your heart.

While we leave room for God to be the sole Judge, the Bible instructs us to meet the needs of those who seek our downfall. On the surface, giving your enemies what to eat and drink may appear very ordinary, but we are told the consequence of our acts: we will heap burning coals on their heads. That is, God will be very justified to demonstrate His righteousness by judging them deservedly.

A godly leader must understand that the topic of revenge carries much spiritual connotation than physical; it must, therefore, be completely conceded to the One who occupies that unseen realm, while we continue to do what is expected of us: walking in love and doing good to all men.

- ◈ 125 -

ALL AUTHORITY IS FROM GOD

*"Let everyone be subject to
the governing authorities, for there is no authority
except that which God has established.
The authorities that exist have been established by God.
Consequently, whoever rebels against the authority
is rebelling against what God has instituted, and those
who do so will bring judgment on themselves."*
Romans 13:1, 2, NIV

Godly leaders don't treat the issue of authority with scant regard. There is a divine order that we must be subject to governing authorities, so any leader that acts contrarily is simply a rebel. One of the reasons governing authorities should be respected is that they don't occupy their offices of their own accord. God, the Governor among nations, puts them there even though man may attempt to circumvent or influence outcomes.

Hence, godly leaders must understand that acknowledging earthly authorities indicates respect for God and His divine order. Those who rebel against such authorities consequently rebel against God Himself and should be prepared to bear the judgement that follows.

Obeying earthly authorities is giving Caesar his just dues. It shows alignment with what God, in His supreme, incontestable wisdom, intends to do through such leaders. It indicates reverence for Him as the Source of all authority.

- 126 -

DO GOOD TOWARDS THOSE IN AUTHORITY

"For rulers hold no terror for those who do right,
but for those who do wrong. Do you want to be free
from fear of the one in authority? Then do what is right,
and you will be commended."
Romans 13:3, NIV

This is a sequel to the immediate past gem. Some individuals deploy sabotage in their engagements with leaders. They instigate and sustain resentment towards those in authority. By contrast, the Bible makes abundantly clear the imperative of doing good towards those in authority.

Achieving the foregoing requires obeying their instructions, for instance, towards national development. As we do so, we won't be needlessly afraid of them. We can rest assured that we won't be beneficiaries of their terror or punishments.

- ◊ 127 -

PAY YOUR DUES

*"This is also why you pay taxes,
for the authorities are God's servants, who give their
full time to governing. Give to everyone what you owe them:
If you owe taxes, pay taxes; if revenue, then revenue;
if respect, then respect; if honor, then honor."*
Romans 13:7, NIV

At this point, I am sure we have come to terms with the interwoven relationship between earthly and heavenly authorities. Godly leaders must understand that they and other earthly leaders are actually God's servants who devote their full time to governing. As such, we have been instructed to give whatever is due to earthly authorities, be it meeting financial obligations or fulfilling moral/social expectations.

Doing so replicates the order that has been instituted in heaven. Godly leaders must lead by example by paying taxes and other monetary requirements, not citing thieving political leaders as an excuse not to do so. They must honour earthly leaders as a result of the consciousness that God actually put them there.

- ◻ 128 -

THE ONLY DEBT IS LOVE

"Let no debt remain outstanding,
except the continuing debt to love one another,
for whoever loves others has fulfilled the law."
Romans 13:8, NIV

"Love does no harm to a neighbor.
Therefore love is the fulfillment of the law."
Romans 13:10, NIV

If there is any debt a godly leader owes people or, specifically, the led, it has to be love! The New Testament ushered in the era of love—we are to love God wholeheartedly and love our neighbours as ourselves. The book of Romans corroborates this by regarding love as fulfilling the requirements of the law passed down to God's children in the Old Testament.

There is not a more secure way than acting in love because it does no wrong. Nothing will discredit your leadership than having deficits recorded against your love walk. Activating love brings peace to ourselves, makes God joyful and fosters harmony with others.

- 💎 129 -

BE CAREFUL OF JUDGEMENT

*"You, then, why do you judge your
brother or sister? Or why do you treat them
with contempt? For we will all stand
before God's judgment seat."*
Romans 14:10, NIV

The demands and delicateness of godly leadership require that we handle judgement with the utmost care. In dispensing justice to all and sundry, we must be very careful to avoid belittling others.

No one who appears before us must be made to feel worthless or beneath consideration. This should be observed with the knowing that both leaders and the led will answer to God on the last day. Godly leaders must not pass up the once-in-a-lifetime opportunity to be a humble, just and considerate umpire. Even those beneath us, no matter the distance in hierarchy, must be treated with respect.

THE BOOK OF

I CORINTHIANS

- 💎 130 -

BOAST ONLY IN GOD

"Therefore, as it is written:
'Let the one who boasts boast in the Lord.'"
I Corinthians 1:31, NIV

"Brothers and sisters, think of what you were
when you were called. Not many of you were wise
by human standards; not many were influential;
not many were of noble birth. But God chose the foolish
things of the world to shame the wise; God chose the
weak things of the world to shame the strong.
God chose the lowly things of this world and the
despised things—and the things that are not
—to nullify the things that are, It is because of him
that you are in Christ Jesus, who has become for us
wisdom from God—that is, our righteousness,
holiness and redemption."
I Corinthians 1:26-30, NIV

Despite all that godly leaders possess, we must constantly reorient ourselves to the important fact that we must boast only in God. Never must our boast come from our personalities, achievements or possessions. When we admit that God chooses the foolish things of this world to confound the wise and the weak things of this world to stun the strong, we will thoroughly understand that it is by His grace, mercy and election that we have assumed the roles of leadership and even ascended its rungs.

Leaders who dwell in self-illusion never end well because there is nothing a man owns unless it is first given to him from above. Like it has been mentioned in a previous gem, godly leaders must imbibe the habit of always giving glory to only God.

- 💎 131 -

YOUR AUDIENCE DETERMINES YOUR DELIVERY

"And so it was with me, brothers and sisters.
When I came to you, I did not come with eloquence
or human wisdom as I proclaimed to you
the testimony about God. We do, however,
speak a message of wisdom among the mature,
but not the wisdom of this age or of the rulers
of this age, who are coming to nothing."
I Corinthians 2:1, 6, NIV

"Brothers and sisters, I could not address
you as people who live by the Spirit but as people
who are still worldly—mere infants in Christ.
I gave you milk, not solid food, for you were not
yet ready for it. Indeed, you are still not ready."
I Corinthians 3:1, 2, NIV

My frequent speaking to diverse audiences could be the reason this gem stands out for me. One of the attributes of any good speaker is the ability to understand that their audience determines their delivery in terms of speech and wisdom.

Although Paul had an excellent education, he had to lay everything connected to that aside so that the Spirit could minister through him as he brought the Gospel to the Gentiles. He ditched worldly wisdom for divine wisdom and commendably so. Certainly, if he had resorted to using worldly wisdom, he would have made the Gospel of no effect, and His teachings wouldn't have been better than intellectual debates between him and leaders of that age.

In addition to that, Paul observed the immaturity of these Christians and decided to offer them a spiritual diet—milk —that they could digest at the time. He knew they would find the strong meat of God's Word incomprehensible at that level of growth. Thus, his target audience informed his approach, delivery and degree of teaching. Godly leaders should emulate Apostle Paul by engaging their audiences with wisdom and speech; that is, based on the right approach and their needs per time.

- 💎 132 -

WORLDLY WISDOM

"For the wisdom of this world
is foolishness in God's sight. As it is written:
'He catches the wise in their craftiness.'"
I Corinthians 3:19, NIV

That it took me so long to understand this particular verse hurts. As leaders, we are conditioned by the modern world to chase knowledge, and there is nothing wrong with that. But the folly in our decision is revealed when we compare worldly wisdom to God's superior, irrevocable wisdom. Put differently, the world's wisdom is foolishness in the light of God's wisdom.

The Yoruba people of the South-Western Region of Nigeria have a particular proverb I like, that describes God as the one who uses the basket to fetch water in order to shame the bucket. In other words, He uses what the world considers foolish to achieve His desires. Upon acknowledging that the standard of this world will always have inadequacies, godly leaders must lean on this heavenly wisdom to achieve tangible results while leading others.

- 💎 133 -

TRUST AND FAITHFULNESS

*"Now it is required that those who
have been given a trust must prove faithful."*
I Corinthians 4:2, NIV

A leader leads due to a major reason: the trust which the led have invested in him. The absence of trust will surely lead to disunity. And in return for the trust they have accorded to leaders, followers expect faithfulness on the part of godly leaders. Faithfulness means remaining unwaveringly loyal to someone or something and putting that loyalty into consistent practice regardless of any circumstances.

Godly leaders must be steadfast in their resolve to adhere to the promise, oath or vow they have undertaken; their exemplary leadership is confirmed in their display of commitment to the people they are contracted to. Leaders who struggle with unfaithfulness are exposed later, if not sooner, causing them disrepute and regression.

- 💎 134 -

ENDURANCE

"We work hard with our own hands.
When we are cursed, we bless; when we are persecuted,
we endure it; when we are slandered, we answer kindly.
We have become the scum of the earth, the garbage
of the world—right up to this moment."
1 Corinthians 4:12, 13, NIV

Endurance is the ability to withstand adversity. In the course of hard work, commitment, integrity and consistency, a leader's life cannot be separated from endurance. Apostle Paul is highly revered today, but we must never gloss over what he experienced in order to deliver the Gospel to Christians back then—the teachings that have now become the Epistles we read for edification, transformation and growth.

He spoke about the sacrifice of manual labour, the curses he endured—which he responded to with kindness, the persecution and slander he suffered and his acknowledgement that he and his fellow leaders had become the world's garbage. Yet, he never backed down from his assignment. Nowhere was it recorded that he complained about the rigours of ministry. When situations turn gloomy, a leader's resilience makes all the difference. Every godly leader must build up a reservoir of endurance as it will be needed for the demanding journey ahead.

- 💎 135 -

BENEFITS

"If we have sown spiritual seed among you,
is it too much if we reap a material harvest
from you? If others have this right of support
from you, shouldn't we have it all the more?
But we did not use this right. On the contrary,
we put up with anything rather than hinder
the gospel of Christ."
I Corinthians 9:11, 12, NIV

"But I have not used any of these rights.
And I am not writing this in the hope that you
will do such things for me, for I would rather die
than allow anyone to deprive me of this boast."
I Corinthians 9:15, NIV

I have seen many leaders who pass up what can be rightfully described as their rights, perks or allowances (e.g. accommodation, transportation, feeding). Such leaders often become so aligned with those they lead, and this disposition gives them a unique voice. Paul, according to Scripture, had paid his dues to a great measure.

By the leading of the Holy Spirit, he traversed so many strange lands and endured the torments of storms, robbers and wild animals. He had gone around sowing spiritual seeds among the Gentile world and, ideally, believed that there should be an accompanying material harvest. Yet, he never exploited this reality so that it wouldn't hinder the Gospel.

He never exercised what was his rights—that which he would not have been criticized for—because he didn't want to constitute a liability to his followers. Godly leaders must also seek to empower themselves such that they won't be needless burdens to those who look to them for succour and guidance.

- 💎 136 -

SELF-DISCIPLINE

"Do you not know that in a race all the runners run,
but only one gets the prize? Run in such a way
as to get the prize. Everyone who competes in the games
goes into strict training. They do it to get a crown
that will not last, but we do it to get a crown
that will last forever. Therefore I do not run
like someone running aimlessly; I do not fight like
a boxer beating the air. No, I strike a blow to my body
and make it my slave so that after I have preached to others,
I myself will not be disqualified for the prize."
I Corinthians 9:24-27, NIV

To buttress the importance of self-discipline, Paul used athletics as an analogy. Leaders are like athletes and must understand that winning the race according to the rules requires strict training and self-discipline. For perspective, an athlete has to deprive himself of some food and bodily enjoyment to be in perfect shape.

Likewise, there will be various demands made of a leader, and any leader who lacks self-discipline will be unable to finish the race and ultimately get the price. Godly leaders must institute a routine which must be strictly followed to achieve certain desired results. Earthly athletes put in the work and reap the rewards. Godly leaders who similarly pay the price through self-discipline will enjoy the dividends of their steadfastness.

- 💎 137 -

THE DYNAMICS OF TEMPTATION

"No temptation has overtaken you
except what is common to mankind.
And God is faithful; he will not let you be
tempted beyond what you can bear. But when you
are tempted, he will also provide a way out
so that you can endure it."
I Corinthians 10:13, NIV

This is one of the most comforting verses of Scripture, especially when a leader is faced with temptation. Temptation is defined as the desire to do something, especially something wrong or unwise. It is the enticement to do evil, an act that one would regret in retrospect.

A leader will face all manner of temptation, including in the areas of sexual immorality and money. And inadequate fortification against such will make even the most well-intentioned leader fall flat. We must never give in to the lie that any temptation is peculiar to anyone, for the Scriptures state otherwise.

What makes the above verse more instructive is how God has assured us that we will not be tempted beyond what we can bear, showcasing His supreme role as Abba. Finally, we can take solace in the fact that when we get tempted, He will also provide a way out so that we can endure it and not be consumed by evil.

- 💎 138 -

GIFTS FOR THE COMMON GOOD

*"Now to each one the manifestation of the Spirit
is given for the common good. To one there is given
through the Spirit a message of wisdom, to another a message
of knowledge by means of the same Spirit, to another faith
by the same Spirit, to another gifts of healing by that one Spirit,
to another miraculous powers, to another prophecy, to another
distinguishing between spirits, to another speaking in different
kinds of tongues, and to still another the interpretation of tongues.
All these are the work of one and the same Spirit, and he distributes
them to each one, just as he determines."*
I Corinthians 12:7-11, NIV

We exist to actualize God's plans and purposes. As godly leaders, we must understand that He usually actualizes these through the instrumentality of interdependence. That is to say, there is not a single leader or individual who possesses all the possible skills to actualize God's will for mankind. Our inadequacies, in one way or the other, ensures we look to others in love and form a mutual relationship of giving and receiving for God to be glorified.

The church in Corinth were schooled in the multidimensional workings of the Spirit of God. Thus, the Spirit blessed some Christians with the manifestation of wisdom, a message of knowledge, faith, the gift of healing, miraculous powers, prophecy, distinguishing spirits, speaking in tongues, and the interpretation of tongues.

As these people used their gifts to complement one another, the church would definitely experience mutual edification and growth. Godly leaders should take their cue from this development, fostering inclusion, interdependence and, ultimately, goal attainment. They should be humble enough to lean on others who may possess what they don't have to get the job done.

- 💎 139 -

BAD COMPANY

"Do not be misled: 'Bad company
corrupts good character.'"
I Corinthians 15:33, NIV

I have studied and understood that, more often than not, many promising leaders have had their bright prospects cut short because of evil company. Hardly will you see such happen to a leader surrounded by well-intentioned people except for those who have allowed pride to make them think they have outgrown the counsel and support of their friends.

Godly leaders must not allow themselves to be misled by self-serving individuals who do not mean well for their leadership. No matter how visionary and spiritual a leader is, it is only a matter of time before the very nature and character of the evil people around him will penetrate his DNA. With that in mind, it is wise to do away with any individual who doesn't align with your godly values before they superimpose their corruption on you in a subtle but dangerous manner.

THE BOOK OF
II CORINTHIANS

- 💎 140 -

YOUR PEOPLE ARE THE EVIDENCE OF YOUR WORKMANSHIP

*"You yourselves are our letter, written on our hearts,
known and read by everyone."*
II Corinthians 3:2, NIV

While achievements or milestones are a testament to commendable leadership, nothing really reveals a leader's sterling qualities like the people he has met, influenced and transformed. In Scripture above, Apostle Paul affirmed that the Corinthians were proof of his thriving ministry to the Gentiles, according to God's design.

It is for this reason that a leader must be conscious of allocating ample time to raising other godly leaders who will replicate his values while they ultimately look like Christ. Do not be the reason lives are languishing in ignorance, poverty and stagnation.

- 💎 141 -

CHASTISEMENT

"Even if I caused you sorrow by my letter,
I do not regret it. Though I did regret it—I see that
my letter hurt you, but only for a little while—yet now
I am happy, not because you were made sorry,
but because your sorrow led you to repentance.
For you became sorrowful as God intended
and so were not harmed in any way by us."
II Corinthians 7:8, 9, NIV

I remember how my father would administer stinging remarks to me when growing up. Although harsh, those comments were targeted towards building my siblings and me, not tearing us down. In the same vein, godly leaders must not be afraid to chastise those they lead, as long as it is done in love, thus serving the purpose of edification and growth. Apostle Paul adopted this strategy with the Corinthians, and it provoked genuine repentance in them.

Godly leaders must never forget that adopting silence, instead of the much-needed chastisement, at any given point in time, may bring more harm than good. It breeds disrespect, disunity and rot. We must not allow the quest to be loved by everyone to make us downplay the necessity of correction—even if it will initially cause pain to the beneficiaries of our rebukes.

- 💎 142 -

ADMINISTERING FREE-WILL GIVING

*"We want to avoid any criticism of the way
we administer this liberal gift. For we are taking pains
to do what is right, not only in the eyes of the Lord
but also in the eyes of man."*
II Corinthians 8:21, NIV

There was a collection for the Lord's people, and the Macedonian churches were extremely generous, surpassing even the expectation of Paul. Titus was nominated to receive the collection, and I like how the godly leader Paul was quick to show the pattern of money administration as per free will giving. He informed his audience about how Titus had not only welcomed his appeal, but was also coming to them with much enthusiasm.

Further, he disclosed that the church—not him—selected Titus for the task, and he did not want any criticism about the way the liberal gift would be administered. This conformed to his desire to be honourable before God and man. Free will or voluntary gifts can be a delicate subject. The administration of such gifts is a banana peel that we must be prepared for so as not to give room to the stinging criticisms of men.

Godly leaders must, therefore, practise wisdom and transparency when handling such gifts. In some cases, it would be appropriate to delegate the handling of such to other people as Paul did to Timothy.

- 💎 143 -

WITNESSED

"This will be my third visit to you.
'Every matter must be established by the testimony
of two or three witnesses.'"
II Corinthians 13:1, NIV

I will explain this gem in two ways: the importance of witnesses and why leaders must make informed decisions only when testimonies are sufficiently corroborated.

In a world where talk is cheap, it is important that a leader institutes a system that ensures witnessing, especially to critical matters. Humans have a tendency to deny, even on oath, things they said or did. It is for this reason legal documents ensure the presence of witnesses to govern contractual dealings and other matters so that in the event of a dispute, there is a method to extract the truth from the lies and denials.

Paul, while speaking to the Corinthian church, advocated that every matter must be established by the testimony of two or three witnesses. In the event of passing judgements or decision-making, a godly leader must encourage receiving testimonies from multiple, trusted witnesses. This prevents bias and solidifies trust between the leader and the led (the trusted witnesses).

THE BOOK OF
GALATIANS

- ◈ 144 -

BEAR THE BURDENS OF OTHERS

*"Carry each other's burdens,
and in this way you will fulfill the law of Christ."*
Galatians 6:2, NIV

God-fearing leaders are burden bearers, not burden givers. Unfortunately, some leaders overburden those they are supposed to be a blessing to. The Galatian church were encouraged to bear each other's burdens, thus fulfilling the law of Christ (walking in love).

Like beasts of burden (e.g. the donkey), leaders must possess the mental fortitude to lift burdens off people's backs. By doing so, we get our burdens lifted off by God and other people who really care.

- ◈ 145 -

TEST YOUR ACTIONS

*"Each one should test their own actions.
Then they can take pride in themselves alone,
without comparing themselves to someone else."*
Galatians 6:4, NIV

Leaders must establish a system of self-analysis, one that allows a rigorous testing of our actions and the intentions that drive them. This honest analysis will help us discern the motive behind our actions and the consequences of such deeds.

Instructively, too, leaders must do away with unhealthy comparison in order to enjoy the uniqueness of our purposes. We must constantly weigh our actions, words and thoughts to see if they indeed bring glory and honour to God.

- ◈ 146 -

SOWING AND REAPING

"Do not be deceived: God cannot be mocked.
A man reaps what he sows."
Galatians 6:7, NIV

The law of sowing and reaping is universal and practical. Practically speaking, you cannot plant mangoes and expect to reap apples. That will amount to self-deceit. Godly leaders must also walk in the consciousness that, in due season, we will reap what we sow in words, thoughts and decision-making.

God, who has no favourites when dispensing rewards, is a rewarder of all men. This is why He has left us with no excuse by empowering us to do just His bidding. For this reason, we must lead with the fear of the Lord and a sense of accountability.

- ◈ 147 -

DO NOT BE WEARY IN DOING GOOD

"Let us not become weary in doing good,
for at the proper time we will reap a harvest
if we do not give up."
Galatians 6:9, NIV

Doing so much good and not getting a deserving acknowledgement can be frustrating, yet the aforementioned portion of Scripture has admonished godly leaders not to become weary in doing good. Adhering to this instruction causes us to reap a due harvest at the right time.

Most leaders give up on this admonition because of what can be interpreted as the slow nature of getting and enjoying the reward, but we must understand that God will test the integrity of our hearts during this period. He will seek to determine whether we are doing good merely for the sake of the harvest or because we truly love Him by obeying His commandments and impacting lives sustainably. The fact that God keeps to His Word should also be enough comfort for us.

THE BOOK OF
EPHESIANS

- ✦ 148 -

SPIRITUAL BLESSINGS

"Praise be to the God and Father of our Lord Jesus Christ,
who has blessed us in the heavenly realms
with every spiritual blessing in Christ."
Ephesians 1:3, NIV

We are not called godly leaders for nothing. It means we are of God; we derive our absolute essence from Him. Against this backdrop, any godly leader that attempts leadership with his own strength and limited knowledge will definitely encounter weariness and frustration. In the letter to the church in Ephesus, Paul praised God for the spiritual blessings His children enjoy. These blessings in Christ can otherwise be regarded as all that pertains to life and Godliness. The awareness of our spiritual positioning makes all the difference as we are able to transport this spiritual reality into our material and tangible world. It distinguishes us from worldly leaders.

God understands the inadequacies of mortal men and, through submission, wants us to access these blessings from His inexhaustible reservoir, for purpose fulfilment. You cannot afford to shortchange yourself and underperform —at least, for the sakes of the destinies connected to you.

- ◈ 149 -

AVOIDING FALSEHOOD

*"Therefore each of you must put off falsehood
and speak truthfully to your neighbor,
for we are all members of one body."*
Ephesians 4:25, NIV

Disturbingly, some leaders are experts in sowing discord by promoting falsehood. Some of them suffer from an inferiority complex and deploy this devious strategy to safeguard their positions. It is why this gem speaks to godly leaders not to be like other individuals who cannot tell the truth at all times.

Handle your subordinates with sincerity because you are members of the same body (e.g. organization, church and so on). No institution flourishes in falsehood because of the distrust it breeds. Let's not hesitate to also charge our followers to always walk in the truth. By upholding the truth at all times, we can be sure of having a good testimony that will outlive our leadership and existence.

- ⬦ 150 -

MANAGING OFFENCES

"'In your anger do not sin':
Do not let the sun go down
while you are still angry, and
do not give the devil a foothold."
Ephesians 4:26, 27, NIV

In leadership, offences are inevitable. Because of the flawed nature of man, you are likely to come across, or work with, people who will render you dissatisfied or angry. And managing the situation poorly will lead to resentment. This is why Scripture warns us to avoid sin when we are angry. It is a thin line that must not be crossed. Jesus, although angry, was careful not to displease God when He sent the money lenders and traders away from the temple. So, while getting angry is justifiable, we must not allow it to be a leash that the devil uses to make us sin.

For this reason, Scripture says we shouldn't let the sun go down while we are still angry. In other words, our anger must not linger, otherwise we will see the devil gain a justifiable foothold in our affairs. This gem speaks about managing our emotions righteously, which can be achieved only by submitting to the Spirit and allowing His fruit to find expression through us.

- ◈ 151 -

AVOID STEALING

*"Anyone who has been stealing must steal no longer,
but must work, doing something useful with their
own hands, that they may have something
to share with those in need."*
Ephesians 4:28, NIV

One of the most uncharitable words often used to describe some leaders is "thief" or "thievery". These insensitive leaders, political and even religious, line their pockets with ill-gotten gains. Eventually, they suffer imprisonment, sack or shame, with some even resorting to suicide.

To avoid this, Apostle Paul encouraged Christians in Ephesus to desist from such an ungodly act and engage in meaningful work so they might have something to share with those in need. In the same vein, I recommend that your leadership journey should be meaningfully engaging. If your kind of leadership permits so, be constructively busy so that you can be economically empowered. Look out for investment opportunities to multiply wealth so that you won't turn a liability to those you serve.

- ◈ 152 -

UNWHOLESOME TALK

*"Do not let any unwholesome talk come out
of your mouths, but only what is helpful for building others up
according to their needs, that it may benefit those who listen."*
Ephesians 4:29, NIV

*"Nor should there be obscenity, foolish talk or coarse joking,
which are out of place, but rather thanksgiving."*
Ephesians 5:4, NIV

A leader's inability to guard his tongue and ensure only edifying and encouraging words emerge from it is one of the most unwelcoming sights. We see leaders who fail to grasp the importance of avoiding unwholesome talk, and this becomes alarming due to their elevated status. I cringe when I hear the obscenity, foolish talk or coarse joking that many professed godly leaders engage.

The world is watching, and many times it is hard to make a distinction between those called by God and those whose master is the devil. Righteous leaders must understand that wise people can discern what leaders hold dear even through their jokes.

For this reason, they shouldn't be found joking about sexual immorality and all manner of impurity, mentioning the name of Jesus flippantly (as is commonly done today), talking down to others, etc. Godly leaders speak to build people and systems up, not destroy them by discouraging them or corrupting them.

- ◈ 153 -

CLEANSE YOUR SPIRIT

"Get rid of all bitterness, rage and anger, brawling and slander, along with every form of malice."
Ephesians 4:31, NIV

Did you know that while some leaders don't struggle with sexual immorality, financial misappropriation, etc., they grapple with the ills mentioned in the portion of Scripture above? Godly leaders must never forget that they are to set examples worthy of emulation in all areas. Those we lead must aspire to be like Jesus because they see His character in us. Consequently, we must get rid of all bitterness, rage and anger, brawling and slander, along with every form of malice.

Holding on to these manifestations of the flesh, on the contrary, will lead to the steady decline and eventual demise of godly leadership. This is because the Spirit of God cannot co-exist with anything that doesn't seek to reveal and glorify Jesus Christ. Also, they contradict the godly injunction of loving God and men, which is the greatest of all commandments.

- ◈ 154 -

EXPOSE EVIL

"Have nothing to do with the fruitless deeds
of darkness, but rather expose them."
Ephesians 5:11, NIV

My kid has a mural at his school that encourages speaking up concerning certain ills such as bullying. I chuckled when reading it out, trying to imagine how the fleshly nature is inclined towards concealing the deeds of darkness.

Many live by the earthly rule of "speak no evil, see no evil and hear no evil". While it is good not to speak evil, godly leaders are enjoined by Scripture to expose any evil that is within their purview. Godly leaders must appreciate that they are called apart and must have absolutely nothing to do with the fruitless deeds of darkness.

We shouldn't turn a blind eye and allow injustice to prevail because a matter doesn't affect us directly. Even if it will lead to our being ostracized, we must stand for what is right. Doing the will of God won't always be comfortable for us anyway.

We must remain so resolute to combat darkness that its perpetrators cannot afford to execute the same under our watch. We are not called the light of the world just for the fun of it. Our illumination should expose anything that allows darkness to hold sway in our environment.

- ◈ 155 -

LIVE WISELY

*"Be very careful, then, how you live—not as unwise
but as wise, making the most of every opportunity,
because the days are evil."*
Ephesians 5:15, 16, NIV

Simply put, godly leaders must never be found in the company of those who lead reckless lives. As Paul revealed in the scriptural reference above, the days are evil. Hell is raging and will deploy every weapon in its arsenal to conquer more souls unto eternal damnation. Knowing this, you cannot afford to live like you don't have limited time on earth. You cannot afford to misapply resources and mismanage people. You cannot afford to underutilize your potential. To do so is to live as unwise. Destinies are connected to your steady ascension and progress. God has invested a lot in you and is counting on you.

Maximizing the opportunities God brings your way is how to live soberly, reverently and carefully. Doing so helps us triumph over evil while we anchor our trust to God alone. Our resolve to live carefully should become an inspiration to those who genuinely desire to imbibe godly values. God is banking on you; posterity will soon be on the scene before you know it. Don't disappoint them.

- ◈ 156 -

HIS WILL

"Therefore do not be foolish,
but understand what the Lord's will is."
Ephesians 5:17, NIV

There is indeed a way that will seem right to some men but will eventually end in destruction. When a leader attempts to lead on his own terms, he will encounter difficulty due to the shortsighted nature of man. The Bible aptly describes this as foolishness.

Godly leaders must strive to thoroughly, although progressively, discern God's will. They mustn't leave their engagements to assumptions or second-guessing. Seeking God's will through submission to the Lord will afford such a leader unusual insight that will spur loyalty and reverence from those being led. Finally, it will ensure you and the led don't end up in the ditch of preventable consequences, as a blind man cannot lead another blind man to a safe destination.

- ◈ 157 -

HONOUR AND SUBMISSION

"Submit to one another out of reverence for Christ."
Ephesians 5:21, NIV

"'Honor your father and mother'
—which is the first commandment with a promise
—'so that it may go well with you and that you may enjoy life
on the earth.' Fathers, do not exasperate your children;
instead, bring them up in the training and instruction of the Lord.
Slaves, obey your earthly masters with respect and fear,
and with sincerity of heart, just as you would obey Christ.
And masters, treat your slaves in the same way.
Do not threaten them, since you know that he who
is both their Master and yours is in heaven,
and there is no favoritism with him."
Ephesians 6:2-5, 9, NIV

"Wives, submit yourselves to your husbands,
as is fitting in the Lord. Husbands, love your wives
and do not be harsh with them. Children,
obey your parents in everything, for this pleases the Lord.
Fathers, do not embitter your children,
or they will become discouraged."
Colossians 3:18-21, NIV

These days, submission is a very delicate subject to discuss, particularly in the light of schools of thought canvassing for gender equality, for instance. Nonetheless, the infallible wisdom of God requires that we submit to humans in authority, from the home to the workplace to church and in government.

Of course, this starts from submitting everything connected to our existence at the feet of the Master. This reverence for Jesus should, therefore, spur us to submit to one another. In the home, the wife is supposed to submit to the husband as proof that she honours the headship/leadership God has conferred on him. Even a man is supposed to submit to his wife through love by handling her with every sense of care, transparency and accountability.

Parents are supposed to honour their children by avoiding anything that can vex the children's souls while they are being raised in the way of the Lord. Young godly leaders are expected to honour their parents, too. Subordinates or followers should submit to their leaders by demonstrating obedience, respect, loyalty and sincerity. Submission is one of the parameters for testing our becoming like the Christ who left His exalted position in heaven to honour His Father while on earth.

- ◈ 158 -

THE ARMOUR OF GOD

"Finally, be strong in the Lord and in his mighty power.
Put on the full armor of God, so that you can take your
stand against the devil's schemes."
Ephesians 6:11, NIV

There is a spiritual armour that is available to all godly leaders, but not all of them put it to effective use. By putting on this full armour, we can take our unwavering stand against the devil's schemes which are targeted towards destroying a leader and disrupting his assignment.

Notably, the armour is comprised of the belt of truth, meaning that godly leaders are expected to give no room to the devil by walking in the truth always. Also, there is the breastplate of righteousness, indicating the importance of serving God through righteous living.

The helmet of salvation indicates that being born again is absolutely necessary to overcome the schemes of darkness. The shield of faith is a reminder that it is impossible to please God without faith. The sword of the Spirit, otherwise called the Word of God, should reignite in every godly leader the consciousness that no one can fulfil destiny and resist the devil outside of the scope of Scripture.

What's more, the gospel of peace fitted to the feet should remind us of our responsibility to preach the Gospel by word of mouth and even our lifestyles everywhere our feet take us. It is important godly leaders understand that the adversary looks for loopholes, hence the emphasis on the "full armour" of God, not some parts.

THE BOOK OF
PHILIPPIANS

– ◈ 159 –

AVOID GRUMBLING

"Do everything without grumbling or arguing,
so that you may become blameless and pure,
'children of God without fault in a warped
and crooked generation.' Then you will shine
among them like stars in the sky."
Philippians 2:14, 15, NIV

The Bible couldn't have explained this much better: avoiding grumbling in your dealings with God and humans effectively establishes blamelessness and purity. Doing so puts you in a position where the prince of this world will have nothing against you, and men can testify to your steadfastness and contentment. Grumbling is born out of lack of contentment and the inclination towards not accepting responsibility for shortcomings – putting the blame on others.

While the children of this world always have complaints upon complaints, we are expected to lead others and administer resources with faith, joy, love, hope and contentment. That is how to walk in the Spirit and not give space to the flesh through grumbling. As the light that we are, that is how to "shine among them like stars in the sky".

- ◈ 160 -

FORGET THE PAST

*"Brothers and sisters, I do not consider myself
yet to have taken hold of it. But one thing I do:
Forgetting what is behind and straining
toward what is ahead."*
Philippians 3:13, NIV

Drawbacks of the past are among the most constraining chains that can keep an individual in a cycle of pain, regret and backwardness. I have had my share of this and, believe me, it truly hinders progress. Like Apostle Paul has admonished, godly leaders must learn to put behind the hurts, mistakes and other unpleasant occurrences of the past so that they can make the most of the now and future.

As is rendered in the English language, it's no use crying over spilt milk. You cannot undo the past, but you must never forget that old things have passed away and all things have become new for those who are truly in Christ Jesus. As a godly leader, therefore, forge ahead to make better decisions and choices. Apostle Paul would put his sordid past of being a persecutor behind so that he could walk with God passionately and present the Gospel to the Gentiles in all truth.

From the language of the verse above, we can discern continuous actions ("forgetting" and "straining"), so this is not a one-off task. Dear godly leader, regardless of how messy and regrettable your past is, you must constantly keep forgetting what is behind and march towards what is ahead. Heed not the devil's lies; greater glory awaits you as you walk with God on a daily basis.

- ◈ 161 -

GENTLENESS

"Let your gentleness be evident to all.
The Lord is near."
Philippians 4:5, NIV

Gentleness was the hallmark of the ultimate Leader—Jesus Christ. We can sense His gentle disposition in His encounter with the Samaritan woman and the adulterous woman, among others. Godly leaders must equally be gentle always; as lambs, we must endeavour not to handle leadership in a brash and combative manner.

A gentle demeanour is a fragrance that makes our lives attractive to those who will care to know the mandate we carry. By contrast, nothing turns people away from a leader than when one appears like a circus clown with a loud disposition towards affairs. Godly leaders should be gentle in their words and actions; remember, the Lord is near.

- ◈ 162 -

ANXIETY

"Do not be anxious about anything,
but in every situation, by prayer and petition,
with thanksgiving, present your requests to God."
Philippians 4:6, NIV

As a leader, this remains one of my favourite verses of the Bible. I particularly like how it encompasses different pathways that replace the hobby (being anxious) of millions of leaders, specifically, and billions of individuals, generally. We live in what may be described as a very stressful world. It, sometimes, becomes so overwhelming when it seems life comes at you like a meteor from space, with imminent impact and little chance for escape.

As a leader, you are bombarded with diverse matters that require your immediate attention. In fact, we have, from the gems in this book, seen a boatload of issues that godly leaders confront head-on. The result of being overwhelmed is often anxiety which means worry over something. The mere fact that some leaders cannot predict the outcomes of their steadfast labour can birth anxiety.

However, God doesn't want His children anxious. Doing so will becloud our ability to make the right calls, leading to irreparable damage in some cases. For this reason, Scripture has admonished godly leaders not to exhibit anxiety for any reason—be it over a trivial or consequential issue.

Instead, we must present our hearts' desires or those troubling situations to God through prayer, petition and thanksgiving. This gem encourages godly leaders to truly demonstrate that they serve a God who cannot be outdone by "the impossible". What is more, it deepens our relationship with Him.

- ◈ 163 -

MEDITATION

"Finally, brothers and sisters, whatever is true,
whatever is noble, whatever is right,
whatever is pure, whatever is lovely,
whatever is admirable—if anything is excellent
or praiseworthy—think about such things."
Philippians 4:8, NIV

The subject matter of meditation has received several interpretations by many Christians. Due to the scarcity of exegesis on the matter, many Christians tend to ignore meditation altogether, believing it is within the exclusive preserve of a select few. However, the Word was given to all Christians, including godly leaders.

Godly leaders must become meditative individuals, thus seeking out time and space for deep reflections and contemplations. As mentioned in Scripture above, our meditations must revolve around some non-negotiable virtues: things that are true, things that are noble, things that are right, things that are pure, things that are lovely, things that are admirable, as well as anything that is excellent and praiseworthy.

As a consequence, godly leaders should avoid meditating on whatever is at variance with the foregoing. Whenever godly leaders' hearts reflect on these parameters, it facilitates clarity, constant gratitude and the unwavering resolve to keep pleasing God as they lead others.

- ◈ 164 -

PRACTICE

"Whatever you have learned or received
or heard from me, or seen in me—put it into practice.
And the God of peace will be with you."
Philippians 4:9, NIV

No doubt, Paul was not merely a nominal Christian. He was one who walked the talk. Indeed, he was worth following only as he followed Christ. As a result of leading an exemplary life, Paul could boldly tell the Christians of his time to emulate his teachings and conduct—he admonished them to put whatever they had learnt, received or heard from him into practice.

As a godly leader, can you confidently make Paul's declaration as stated in Scripture above? Will this deepen the harmony in your circle or birth anarchy? This verse should pierce the heart of every leader and spur them to assess their lifestyle. With that, adjustments can be made to ensure their misconduct or inadequacies don't rub off on the led.

- ◈ 165 -

THE SECRET OF CONTENTMENT

"I know what it is to be in need,
and I know what it is to have plenty.
I have learned the secret of being content
in any and every situation, whether well fed
or hungry, whether living in plenty or in want.
I can do all this through him who gives me strength."
Philippians 4:12, 13, NIV

As another portion of Scripture renders the above verse this way, godliness with contentment is great gain. Contentment affords a godly leader the opportunity to attain the peak of purpose fulfilment. It is the quest for more and more that often sucks most leaders into a vortex that they are unable to escape from. When a leader is content, by contrast, it is hard for him to be bribed or bought over; he is able to make the right decisions without fear or favour.

Paul knew what it meant to be in need and the feeling that comes with abundance. Most importantly, he confessed his resolve to demonstrate contentment in all situations through divine strengthening. This proves that you cannot attain the level of contentment that is required of you by your own strength. Contentment can, therefore, be experienced when you solely depend on God who gives His beloved ones the ability to please Him in all circumstances.

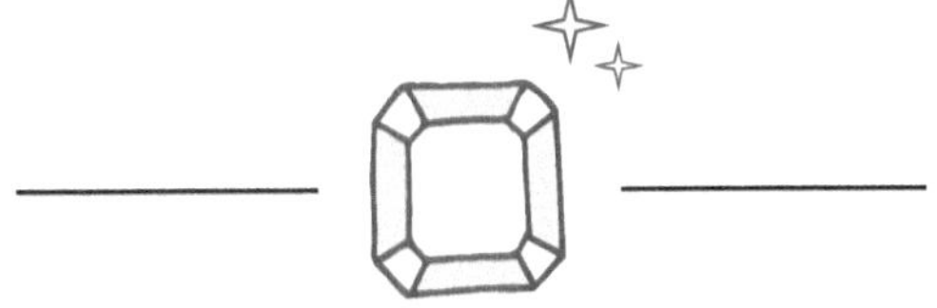

THE BOOK OF
COLOSSIANS

- ⬦ 166 -

WORLDLY PHILOSOPHY

"See to it that no one takes you captive
through hollow and deceptive philosophy,
which depends on human tradition
and the elemental spiritual forces of this
world rather than on Christ."
Colossians 2:8, NIV

Our world is full of all types of philosophies. It almost appears like an avalanche released on the earth, with all manner of expressions (deceptions sponsored by the elemental forces of this world) given amplification by the media of the day.

Every godly leader must understand the fact that the ways of the world are in direct conflict with that of the Kingdom; and because of the influence that leaders command, they are prime targets of these philosophies. It is easier to indoctrinate a multitude with evil philosophies by simply winning over their leader. Scripture above reveals that this is a battle of the mind, and anyone or thing that rules the mind rules the body and soul as well.

Godly leaders must ensure their minds and the minds of the led are not held captive by these philosophies that cause men to stray away from the truth. We are to lead from the forefront with nothing but the ever-relevant Word of God.

- 💎 167 -

HEAVENLY PERSPECTIVES

*"Set your minds on things above,
not on earthly things."*
Colossians 3:2, NIV

The allure of this world can be so tempting for a godly leader. Thankfully, nothing catches God unawares. So, He has strongly instructed us to set our minds on heavenly, not earthly, things. Of course, this doesn't mean we should live as though God doesn't care about how we conduct ourselves on earth.

Rather, we are to accord attention to heavenly perspectives that make for eternal life and not seek joy, contentment or validation from earthly, material things that will perish eventually. As leaders, our eyes must constantly be on heaven and all it holds for us.

- 🔲 168 -

FAIRNESS

*"Masters, provide your slaves with what
is right and fair, because you know that
you also have a Master in heaven."*
Colossians 4:1, NIV

The conversation about how leaders are supposed to correctly remunerate those that serve them is a topic I am confronted with during training sessions with organizations. The question of right and fair will always trigger debates, and my humble submission is that no single glove can fit all situations because of their uniqueness.

For this reason, Scripture instructs masters or leaders to deal with their employees or followers in all righteousness and fairness. With the Spirit empowering us, godly leaders should not cheat and oppress the led. This is how to exalt God before men so that He can draw them towards Him.

- 🔲 169 -

HANDLING OUTSIDERS

*"Be wise in the way you act toward outsiders;
make the most of every opportunity."*
Colossians 4:5, NIV

The story of how Abraham entertained strangers, which this book addressed in its Old Testament aspect, and the portion of Scripture above solidify the importance of hospitality. Godly leaders must handle outsiders with wisdom. The Gospel that will win many to the Kingdom of God must be delivered by reflecting the accommodating nature of the Christ we profess.

Although some people may abuse this, this book has addressed the importance of acting in accordance with God's pleasure come what may. How we treat outsiders will, to a considerable extent, reveal if we are truly Christ's.

- ◻ 170 -

CONVERSATIONS

"Let your conversation be always full of grace,
seasoned with salt, so that you may know
how to answer everyone."
Colossians 4:6, NIV

Here, godly leaders are instructed that their conversations must be grace-filled and seasoned with salt. By implication, the utterances of godly leaders must be rich in the grace of our Lord Jesus Christ—the same grace with which you have been called to leadership.

Just as salt brings out the taste of food, your conversations must cause people to taste of God's character—love, mercy, purity and the like. As salt adds value to food, your conversation must add value to your listeners. All in all, our conversations must be geared towards the edification, not the destruction, of people.

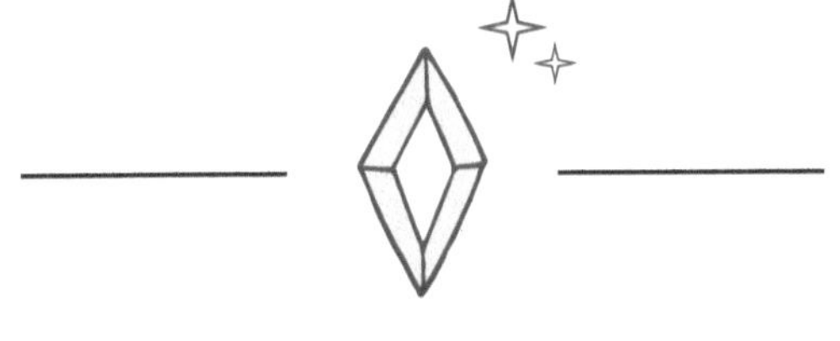

THE BOOK OF

I THESSALONIANS

- ◈ 171 -

LEADING A QUIET LIFE

*"And to make it your ambition to lead
a quiet life: You should mind your own business
and work with your hands, just as we told you,
so that your daily life may win the respect of outsiders
and so that you will not be dependent on anybody."*
I Thessalonians 4:11, 12, NIV

Regardless of the volume of noise and distractions the world offers, godly leaders are expected to lead a quiet life. This can be achieved by Paul's recommendation of minding one's own business and working with one's hands. Doing so will ensure we don't become a liability to others, and we earn other people's regard.

This is why godly leaders must not be found in every gathering and at the centre of every conversation. You cannot be everywhere if you truly are leading a visionary life. Any leader who disregards this gem will, sooner or later, experience diminishing returns.

- ◊ 172 -

ACKNOWLEDGING HARD WORKERS

"Now we ask you, brothers and sisters,
to acknowledge those who work hard among you,
who care for you in the Lord and who admonish you.
Hold them in the highest regard in love because
of their work. Live in peace with each other."
I Thessalonians 5:12, 13, NIV

Many leaders, including godly leaders, fall short of their responsibility to acknowledge the hard work of the led. For whatever reasons, they are miserly when it comes to paying compliments or offering financial rewards to their followers. By contrast, Paul admonished that hardworking people should be accorded honour.

As a godly leader, when last did you generously dish out sincere compliments to hard workers in your circle? Besides paying them salaries, have you ever thought of appreciating their diligence and consistency by giving them financial incentives? Do you truly hold this special group of individuals in the highest regard?

Believe me, it becomes underwhelming when anyone begins to feel unappreciated. Therefore, godly leaders mustn't joke with engaging the necessary steps that make their followers aware that their consistent labours of love have not gone unnoticed.

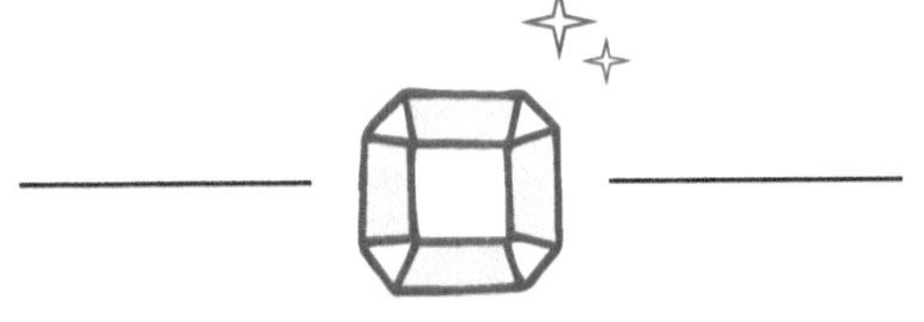

THE BOOK OF
II THESSALONIANS

- ⊞173 -

DEAL DECISIVELY WITH INDOLENCE

"Even when we were with you, we gave you this rule:
'The one who is unwilling to work shall not eat.'"
II Thessalonians 3:10, NIV

The above portion of Scripture reveals that the leaders then were cautious not to enable or consent to a culture of laziness. Godly leaders must also ensure that their spheres of influence are governed by the rule of rewarding only hard workers.

We should, therefore, encourage meritocracy and frown upon any system that encourages the led to become dependents on handouts. A system of hard work must be the driving force of our leadership style, and this must cascade down for everyone to see and abide by.

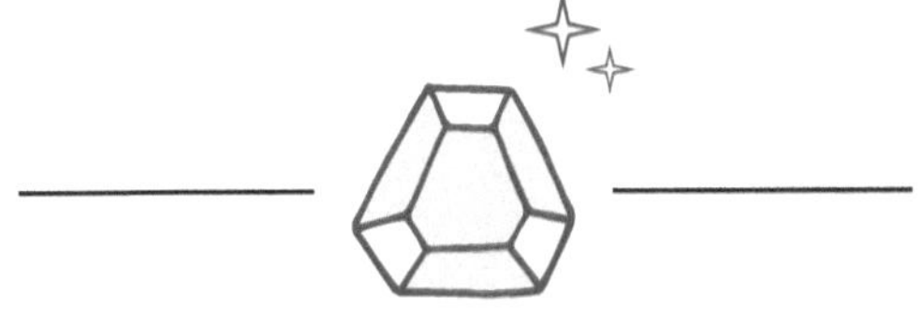

THE BOOK OF
I TIMOTHY

– ◈ 174 –

PRAYER FOR LEADERS

"I urge, then, first of all, that petitions, prayers,
intercession and thanksgiving be made for all
people— for kings and all those in authority,
that we may live peaceful and quiet lives in all
godliness and holiness."
I Timothy 2:1, 2, NIV

This Scripture reveals how Paul sought true leadership, thus reminding the church about how Jesus modelled authentic leadership. The first few lines of this letter were an admonition that all manner of petitions, prayers, intercession and thanksgiving should be made for all people, including kings and those in authority. This was targeted at ensuring that people could lead peaceful and quiet lives in all godliness and holiness. This is a sacred duty that godly leaders must uphold passionately.

Prayer spurs God to empower leaders to govern people with wisdom, thus ensuring God's agenda is not frustrated or thwarted. Our consistent intercessions on behalf of other leaders will ensure that people from all walks of life can go about their activities in peace and righteousness. They are for our collective benefit.

- ◈ 175 -

WHAT LEADERS CAN LEARN FROM DEACONS

"Here is a trustworthy saying:
Whoever aspires to be an overseer
desires a noble task."
I Timothy 3:1, NIV

"If I am delayed, you will know how people
ought to conduct themselves in God's household,
which is the church of the living God, the pillar
and foundation of the truth."
I Timothy 3:15, NIV

"Since an overseer manages God's household,
he must be blameless—not overbearing,
not quick-tempered, not given to drunkenness,
not violent, not pursuing dishonest gain.
Rather, he must be hospitable, one who loves
what is good, who is self-controlled,
upright, holy and disciplined."
Titus 1:7, 8, NIV

The Bible specifically highlights certain qualities that overseers and deacons must possess, and I am of the opinion that godly leaders should imbibe them. The first portion of Scripture affirms that whoever aspires to be an overseer desires a noble task, just like whoever aspires to lead others actually desires what is noble.

Such a godly leader should be above reproach, should be faithful to their marriage vows, should demonstrate self-control, should be respectable, should be hospitable, should be an exemplary teacher, and should avoid drunkenness, violence, quarrels and the lust for money.

Not only that, such an individual must command respect while leading his own family and mustn't be a recent convert so that he wouldn't be overcome by pride. This latter part reveals that any leadership role, ecclesiastical or secular, requires the maturity that comes with experience. The leader must have an untainted reputation. They must avoid malice and exhibit trustworthiness in everything. These detailed qualifications are, in my considered opinion, required for any leader to execute their roles effectively to bring glory to God.

- ◈176 -

GODLINESS

*"Have nothing to do with godless myths
and old wives' tales; rather, train yourself to be godly.
For physical training is of some value, but godliness
has value for all things, holding promise for
both the present life and the life to come."*
I Timothy 4:8, NIV

Godliness is fast becoming outdated or unfashionable among some leaders; they consider it a character trait that belongs to the early church, not our modern era. Quite the contrary, God's ways and demands will remain forever unchanged.

Godly leaders operating in this age must have nothing to do with what the Bible calls godless myths and old wives' tales. These can be interpreted as worldly things that bear no merit. Instead, we are to exercise ourselves in godliness which benefits us immensely and every time. Indeed, no one can ever go wrong by demonstrating godliness. Doing so is to the advantage of godly leaders while on earth and even in the endless age that is to come.

- ◈177 -

AGE

Although it was stressed before that leadership requires maturity that comes with experience, room should, nonetheless, be created for up-and-coming leaders to flourish. Any young leader reading this gem shouldn't allow anyone to look down on them because of their age and inexperience.

Instead, they should busy themselves with modelling righteousness in the following areas: speech, conduct, love, faith and purity. Use the energy, creativity and fearlessness that come with youth to your advantage. Doing so is the reason we have young people emerging to lead conversations and champion causes.

Regardless of whether you are in your late teens, your twenties or your thirties, you shouldn't be left out of the mandate to impact lives with the capacity God has gifted you.

- ◈178 -

WATCH YOUR LIFE

"Watch your life and doctrine closely.
Persevere in them, because if you do, you will
save both yourself and your hearers."
I Timothy 4:16, NIV

Godly leaders must pay close attention to their lives and the doctrines instilled in them so that they and their followers won't veer off God's demands of them. The plague of distraction will confront even the most prepared leaders. Its sole, destructive purpose is to ensure we take our eyes off our lives and the doctrines that drive them.

If you fall for this trap, it is only a matter of time before you begin to imbibe the wrong doctrines and live unrighteously. The consequences of the foregoing on your life, your family, the workplace and your followers are better imagined than experienced. For preservation's sake, don't be too busy to keep imbibing the right doctrines so that you can live rightly until God calls you home.

- ◇179 -

DEMOGRAPHICS

"Do not rebuke an older man harshly,
but exhort him as if he were your father.
Treat younger men as brothers, older women
as mothers, and younger women as sisters,
with absolute purity."
I Timothy 5:1, 2, NIV

It is a no-brainer that leadership requires handling people of different backgrounds, genders and age grades. Managing this diversity, especially in the case of a young leader like Timothy, requires wisdom and maturity.

As such, Scripture admonishes that godly leaders should treat older males as they would do to their fathers and younger males as they would do to their brothers. Additionally, older women should be treated as one's mother while younger women should be treated as one's sisters, with absolute purity. In other words, godly leaders should never take advantage of young women. Achieving all of this will make leadership more of a fulfilling task than merely a laborious undertaking.

- ◈180 -

WHO'S WORSE THAN AN INFIDEL?

*"Anyone who does not provide for
their relatives, and especially for their own household,
has denied the faith and is worse than an unbeliever."*
I Timothy 5:8, NIV

Leaders, by virtue of their calling, are meant to be providers and should never be found doing anything that robs them of the ability to provide. In fact, Scripture reveals the severity of not fulfilling this role by likening such an individual to an unbeliever or an infidel who doesn't have a stake in the inheritance of God.

Practically speaking, leaders must spiritually, financially, emotionally and intellectually provide for their immediate families, their relatives, and those they lead. Acting contrarily is simply abusing the grace or election of God upon your life.

- ◈181 -

CONTENTMENT

"But godliness with contentment is great gain."
I Timothy 6:6, NIV

"For we brought nothing into the world,
and we can take nothing out of it. But if we have
food and clothing, we will be content with that.
Those who want to get rich fall into temptation
and a trap and into many foolish and harmful desires
that plunge people into ruin and destruction.
For the love of money is a root of all kinds of evil.
Some people, eager for money, have wandered from
the faith and pierced themselves with many griefs."
I Timothy 6:7-10, NIV

The harsh realization of the vanity of the things around us is enough to make us embrace contentment. Unfortunately, that is not the case with every leader. In spite of his access to women and wealth, Solomon declared everything "vanity upon vanity".

In Scripture above, great gain is simply defined as combining godliness with contentment. Take note that the Bible didn't state that godliness with contentment will "give" you great gain. Actually, godliness with contentment "is" already great gain! For this reason, godly leaders should always express contentment with whatever God commits to them per season.

This is how not to allow the love of money, which is the root of all evil, to drive us towards indulging in ungodly practices that end up in sorrow. It is sad that the love of money has made some well-intentioned leaders turn devilish. The earlier we understand that only the blessing of God makes rich and adds no sorrow, the more we will embrace contentment and not make a shipwreck of our faith!

- ◈ 182 -

GUARD WHAT IS IN YOUR CARE

"Timothy, guard what has been
entrusted to your care. Turn away from godless
chatter and the opposing ideas of what is
falsely called knowledge."
I Timothy 6:20, NIV

Guarding what is kept in our care is a sign of faithfulness and the high expectation of leaders. First, we must dutifully guard the treasures of godly mindsets embedded in our hearts. We mustn't trade scriptural perspectives for anything in this world!

Next, we are to cater for the individuals God has entrusted to us with the dexterity of a loving shepherd. This is extremely important because every individual created in

His image matters to Him! We cannot afford to be careless in our approach to leadership. Jesus, our model Leader, gave an account of all His disciples, including Judas who betrayed Him.

THE BOOK OF
II TIMOTHY

- ◈ 183 -

LOYALTY AND DISLOYALTY

*"You know that everyone in the province of Asia
has deserted me, including Phygelus and Hermogenes."*
II Timothy 1:15, NIV

One thing I can confidently declare from the rooftop is that leaders will encounter loyalty and disloyalty, regardless of the uniqueness of their journeys. While Paul enjoyed loyalty from the likes of Timothy, his mentee, he had to endure disloyalty in the form of desertion from the likes of Phygelus and Hermogenes. This must have been heartbreaking for Paul.

Additionally, he enjoyed loyalty from the household of Onesiphorus who refreshed him and was not ashamed of his chains. In fact, Onesiphorus looked for Paul and was of immense help to the apostle in Ephesus.

Even Jesus, God made flesh, experienced His fair share of loyalty and disloyalty. Godly leaders must prepare their minds that the humans that will cross paths with them will dish out from only two bowls—loyalty or disloyalty.

- ◈ 184 -

THE VICTOR'S CROWN

"No one serving as a soldier gets entangled
in civilian affairs, but rather tries to please
his commanding officer. Similarly, anyone who
competes as an athlete does not receive the victor's
crown except by competing according to the rules."
II Timothy 2:5, NIV

One of the qualities of a competent soldier is the ability to focus on the task at hand; in fact, Apostle Paul affirmed that soldiers are so bent on pleasing their master that they don't bother themselves with civilian matters. This discipline should be emulated by leaders who desire to win.

A godly leader also has a commanding Leader in the person of Jesus Christ, and our chief aim is to please Him by not getting entangled with matters that do not concern our divine mandates. Like an athlete who receives the victor's crown for competing according to the rules, godly leaders will definitely be acknowledged and rewarded for running the race set before them (executing their divine assignments). They are to achieve the same by adhering to the rules for executing their assignments from God's Word.

- ✧ 185 -

SPECIAL PURPOSES

*"In a large house there are articles not only of gold
and silver, but also of wood and clay; some are for special
purposes and some for common use. Those who cleanse
themselves from the latter will be instruments for
special purposes, made holy, useful to the Master
and prepared to do any good work."*
II Timothy 2:20, 21, NIV

As in the case of vessels which serve different purposes—some, special; some, common—in a house, Scripture makes us understand that leaders can serve different purposes based on their capacity.

Therefore, godly leaders who cleanse themselves of all manifestations of dishonour will not serve common purposes. Because they are holy, they will become God's instruments for special purposes. Just like God gave the Israelites the liberty to choose between life and death, the onus is on us to determine if we will be vessels unto honour or dishonour.

I implore every leader to choose being an honourable vessel that serves special purposes by cleansing themselves of every defilement of the flesh and the spirit. Only by doing so will effective and optimum leadership be established. Deep introspection must be carried out to ascertain where defilement lies in our hearts and lifestyles, thus subjecting our vessels to the washing by the word of God.

- ◈ 186 -

AVOID FOOLISH AND STUPID ARGUMENTS

*"Don't have anything to do with foolish
and stupid arguments, because you know
they produce quarrels."*
II Timothy 2:23, NIV

Engaging in baseless arguments is one of the surest ways to remain unproductive and get defiled spiritually. As such, godly leaders must steer clear of this endeavour that produces quarrels—the devil's tools of distraction.

You can't function optimally and maximize human resources when you are indulging in quarrelling. Doing so contradicts God's expectation of you that your words should always be full of grace and seasoned with salt.

- ◈ 187 -

PERSECUTION IS A NECESSITY

*"In fact, everyone who wants to live
a godly life in Christ Jesus will be persecuted."*
II Timothy 3:12, NIV

Paul, from his time of conversion, lived a life of painful persecution. Similarly, this gem reminds us that everyone, including godly leaders, who embraces godliness will suffer persecution like our Lord Jesus Christ. We must be ready to carry our cross like He did. We should note that the same world which despised Him won't change their perception of us overnight.

This expected attack becomes more apparent when you are a prominent godly leader. Your faith will be tested time and again as the devil will raise adversaries to persecute you. This reality should prepare you for what lies ahead and not instil fear in you. Recall that you have the spirit of power and love plus a sound mind, not the spirit of fear.

All in all, you must be of good cheer because Jesus has overcome the world for your sake. You are not without help, godly leader. Keep soldiering on.

- ◈ 188 -

SCRIPTURE IS A MAP

"All Scripture is God-breathed and is useful
for teaching, rebuking, correcting
and training in righteousness."
II Timothy 3:16, NIV

Since times past, Scripture has been subjected to scathing criticisms, and the reason is not hard to discern: there is no other book that comprises the requirements for genuine living besides the Bible. For this reason, the devil is fighting aggressively to ensure that the Bible is relegated to the back burner in social settings, homes, etc.

Scripture is a map that helps all believers, including godly leaders, to navigate life without succumbing to trial and error. Nothing else in existence is as accurate and detailed about what has happened, what is happening and what will happen.

With this in mind, godly leaders must believe that the entire Scriptures are inspired by God and are useful for four things: for teaching, for rebuking, for correcting and for training in righteousness. Settling for anything else or less is disregarding or undermining the GPS with which you should get to God's preordained destination for you.

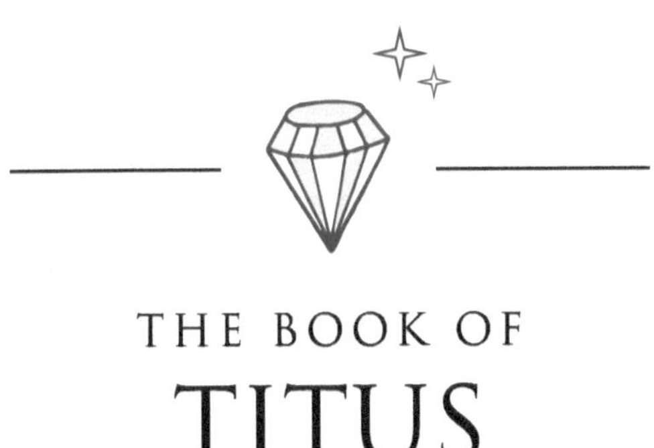

THE BOOK OF
TITUS

- 💎 189 -

DIVISIVENESS

*"Warn a divisive person once, and then warn
them a second time. After that, have nothing to do
with them. You may be sure that such people are warped
and sinful; they are self-condemned."*
Titus 3:10, 11, NIV

Divisive individuals are known for sowing discord; they are never happy seeing calm waters. Here, godly leaders are taught how to handle these persons. We are to warn them once after receiving credible intel about their misconduct. If the first rebuke doesn't achieve the desired effect, we should warn them a second time. And when they refuse to turn over a new leaf, we should have nothing to do with them afterwards.

The Bible has taught us how to handle such people because they are sinful and possess the ability to destroy the fruits of the labours of multiple years. It is your responsibility to spot them and handle them accordingly.

THE BOOK OF
PHILEMON

- ◈ 190 -

FORGIVENESS

"That I appeal to you for my son Onesimus,
who became my son while I was in chains.
Formerly he was useless to you, but now
he has become useful both to you and to me.
So if you consider me a partner, welcome him
as you would welcome me. If he has done you
any wrong or owes you anything, charge it to me."
Philemon 1:10, 11, 17, 18, NIV

Paul felt compelled to write a letter of appeal over Onesimus who had previously been the slave of Philemon. As a slave, Onesimus had run away from his master. He would later be converted, and he helped Paul in prison. Eventually, Paul decided to send him back and have him reconciled to his master. He sought Philemon's forgiveness and promised to stand as a surety if Onesimus had done anything wrong, or he was indebted to his master.

This reveals that forgiveness must be a constant feature in the life of a godly leader. Here, Paul taught us a crucial aspect of the Lord's Prayer: walking in love by forgiving others like God has pardoned our wrongdoings and guilt. Godly leaders should, therefore, make room for hurt and offences, and be prepare to forgive others.

THE BOOK OF
HEBREWS

- ◈ 191 -

MAXIMIZING THE WORD

"For the word of God is alive and active.
Sharper than any double-edged sword, it penetrates
even to dividing soul and spirit, joints and marrow;
it judges the thoughts and attitudes of the heart."
Hebrew 4:12, NIV

Walking in the understanding of God's Word is the difference between walking in success or wallowing in defeat. Godly leaders must understand that the Word of God shouldn't be merely regarded as "it" like magazines, novels and other books. God's Word is actually living because it is Christ Jesus Himself! From Genesis to Revelations, Scripture reveals and testifies about Jesus. The Word is alive and active. Consequently, it can address any situation.

Further, Hebrews affirms the Word's matchless cutting edge—it cannot be matched by the sharpest of two-edged swords. The Word can penetrate even what is seemingly inseparable to effect the necessary adjustments. By extension, a godly leader ought to assess their heart's posture with the supremacy and infallibility of God's Word. By doing so, you can discern whether your loyalty is to God alone, or you have somehow managed to be friends with God and the world simultaneously.

- ◈ 192 -

MERCY AND GRACE

*"Let us then approach God's throne of grace
with confidence, so that we may receive mercy
and find grace to help us in our time of need."*
Hebrews 4:16, NIV

It is not out of place to have godly leaders who are at a loss for what steps to take at a particular juncture. In some instances, it may be that the leader lacks the required strength or resources to implement an initiative. Not to worry, godly leaders are admonished to approach God's throne of grace with the confidence that God can be trusted at all times.

We do this simply because we want to be beneficiaries of His grace and mercy needed for the season. By the way, leaders must understand that "coming confidently" is not the same as "coming arrogantly". As such, we must approach God with the consciousness that He is to be submitted to and not ordered around like a slave. He—not we—is the Boss in the relationship. He calls the shots. He dishes out the terms and conditions, and you must humble yourself under His mighty hand before you experience exaltation above that issue you're currently grappling with.

And after victory has been established, you must never forget to ascribe all the glory to Him by making people realize that you couldn't have achieved whatever it is by your limited strength and intellect.

- ◈ 193 -

DEALING GENTLY

"He is able to deal gently with those
who are ignorant and are going astray,
since he himself is subject to weakness."
Hebrew 5:2, NIV

Here, the Bible admonishes godly leaders to deal with ignorant people gently. These are people who would have acted better if they had known better. The same disposition should be experienced by those going astray. They shouldn't be subjected to force or any other measure that can harden them further.

To do the foregoing is to act like Christ who, although sinless and blameless, understood the temptations and flaws of humanity when He became flesh. You are to exhibit gentleness sponsored by compassion, knowing full well that you also have weaknesses you are currently trusting God to empower you to overcome.

- ◈ 194 -

GOD'S WILL

"Then I said, 'Here I am—it is written about
me in the scroll—I have come
to do your will, my God.'"
Hebrews 10:7, NIV

Godly leaders understand that there is man's will, and there is God's will. Many resort to leaning on their own understanding; and, while they may achieve their definition of success, they won't experience fulfilment. This is simply because God's sovereign will is without error. You shouldn't expect that a television, for instance, can function maximally outside of its maker's instructions.

Similarly, no human can fulfil a purpose outside of God's thoughts and plans. Although God may strategically deploy adversity at some junctures of one's life to strengthen one, one can rest assured that no godly leader has ever regretted fully embracing God's will to execute their mandate of authority.

- ◈ 195 -

FAITH

"And without faith it is impossible to please God,
because anyone who comes to him must believe that
he exists and that he rewards those who earnestly seek him."
Hebrews 11:6, NIV

"And what more shall I say? I do not have time
to tell about Gideon, Barak, Samson and Jephthah,
about David and Samuel and the prophets, who through
faith conquered kingdoms, administered justice,
and gained what was promised; who shut the mouths
of lions, quenched the fury of the flames, and escaped
the edge of the sword; whose weakness was turned
to strength; and who became powerful in battle
and routed foreign armies."
Hebrews 11:33, 34, NIV

We have, at one point or the other, been exposed to conversations around faith, its existence, its importance and the results it can command, yet we find many godly leaders not fully embracing faith. Faith is simply the ability to completely surrender one's trust to, and dependability on, God.

All godly leaders must first understand that it is absolutely impossible to please God without faith. This is in furtherance of the fact that anyone who approaches Him must understand that He is—He exists; He is truly the

"I am that I am"—and He rewards those who seek Him diligently.

Scripture provides us with examples of godly leaders that attained uncommon heights in leadership because of their unalloyed faith in God: Gideon, Barak, Samson, Jephthah, David, Samuel and the prophets. By implication, we have more than enough people to learn from. A faithless leader, on the other hand, will eventually be condemned to the dustbin of history.

- ◈ 196 -

WEIGHT AND SIN

*"Therefore, since we are surrounded by such
a great cloud of witnesses, let us throw off everything
that hinders and the sin that so easily entangles.
And let us run with perseverance the race
marked out for us,"*
Hebrew 12:1, NIV

The Bible couldn't have been more straightforward. Here, godly leaders are instructed to rid themselves of whatever hinders them (weights) and the sins that can easily ensnare them. Weights may not be obvious sins, but they are destructive nonetheless. Examples of such are worry, fear, doubt, ungodly ambition, the wrong relationships (they

282

may not necessarily be ungodly). They are burdens that will slow you down from achieving God's purpose at His ordained pace.

Sins include unrighteous deeds like sexual immorality, envy, lying, etc. and the faulty mindsets that sponsor them. They entangle one, thus leaving one in bondage to their evil consequences. After letting go of the weights and sins that so easily entangle, we are encouraged to run with perseverance the race marked out for us. Here, I must emphasize how important it is for you not to run another man's race. As in the case of athletics, intruding into another man's lane will get you disqualified by God, causing someone else to occupy your spot. No one in their right senses wants to experience this, so godly leaders must maintain their lanes with a never-say-die attitude.

- ◈ 197 -

YOU HAVE A PRECEDENT

*"Consider him who endured such
opposition from sinners, so that you will
not grow weary and lose heart."*
Hebrew 12:3, NIV

In law, the importance of a precedent is something that cannot be overemphasized. It gives a level of certainty of the outcome of proceedings. Therefore, lawyers are able to research and build their cases by learning from similar situations that have transpired before.

In our leadership journey, we should consider the precedent of Jesus' disposition towards His adversaries so that we won't become discouraged as regards pleasing God. The firm but undeniable truth is that those who were here before us, including Jesus, have proved that we have no excuse not to overcome any form of adversity. If they surmounted the strategy of the devil to make them lose heart, we should, too, by God's grace.

- ✦ 198 -

REBUKE AND DISCIPLINE

"And have you completely forgotten this word
of encouragement that addresses you as a father
addresses his son? It says, 'My son, do not make light
of the past Lord's discipline, and do not lose heart when
he rebukes you, because the Lord disciplines the one
he loves, and he chastens everyone he accepts as his son.'
Endure hardship as discipline; God is treating you
as his children. For what children are not disciplined
by their father? If you are not disciplined—and everyone
undergoes discipline—then you are not legitimate,
not true sons and daughters at all."
Hebrews 12:5-8, NIV

"No discipline seems pleasant at the time,
but painful. Later on, however, it produces a harvest
of righteousness and peace for those who
have been trained by it."
Hebrew 12:11, NIV

Discipline is a hard pill to swallow for many leaders because they are accustomed to receiving only praise and accolades. Godly leaders must be humble to acknowledge and accept God's rebuke and discipline which are an outpouring of His love. We must perceive God's discipline from the lenses of a loving father who is trying to ensure His child becomes the best version of himself—a version that is fully conformed to the image of Christ. We shouldn't make light of His rebukes because they reveal our folly and inadequacies.

The litmus test of your standing with God, as a godly leader, is undergoing His discipline; in the absence of this, you are an illegitimate child that will make a reckless leader. After God's discipline has achieved its purpose of ridding us of all impurities, it will produce a harvest of righteousness and peace in our lives.

- ⬦ 199 -

HONOURABLE LIVING

*"Pray for us. We are sure that we have a clear conscience
and desire to live honorably in every way."*
Hebrew 13:18, NIV

It is worrying that some leaders don't take being honourable seriously when, in the actual sense, it is the beauty and crown of a leader. In the portion of Scripture above, Apostle Paul talked about having a clear conscience which is a state where one's heart harbours no negativity or ill-will, and one deals righteously with God and men. This should always be the watchword of godly leaders.

Secondly, it can be noted that godly leaders must carry the desire to live honourably in every way. Of course, this includes honouring all men—young and old, male and female. Leading an honourable life is irresistible. Men cannot help but notice you.

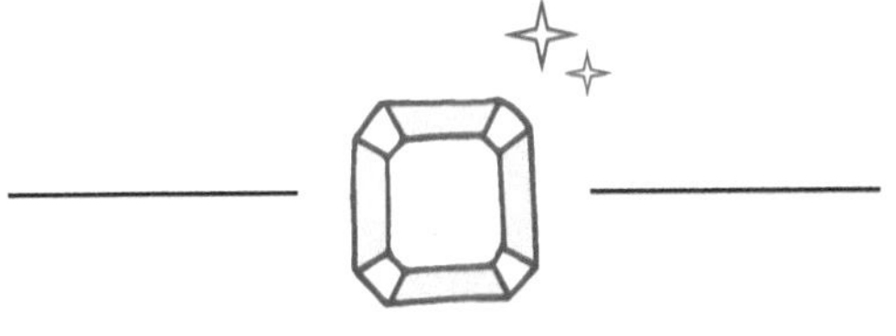

THE BOOK OF
JAMES

- 200 -

THE RESULT OF TESTS

"Because you know that the testing of your
faith produces perseverance. Let perseverance finish
its work so that you may be mature and complete,
not lacking anything."
James 1:4, NIV

No godly leader will be spared of the season of tests or trials; in some cases, it will take the assurance of God not to make you doubt your calling and even yourself. Your faith, just like that of other believers, will surely be put to the test.

Thankfully, God doesn't allow circumstances to occur just for happening's sake. Everything has a larger purpose and a meaning which catapult man to a glorious destination. The very testing of our faith is meant to produce perseverance which is fulfilling all righteousness (doing what is right simply because it is right) despite the difficulties and delays experienced in achieving success.

In turn, when perseverance has fulfilled its purpose completely, you will experience maturity and completeness. At this point, you will experience a greater dimension of God's glory, and it will be obvious to everyone that nothing or nobody, besides God, commands lordship over your life.

- ◻ 201 -

WISDOM CAN BE SOUGHT

*"If any of you lacks wisdom, you should ask God,
who gives generously to all without finding fault,
and it will be given to you."*
James 1:5, NIV

Although wisdom has been mentioned over and over again in this book, this is a timely reminder that godly leaders must never forget that worldly wisdom cannot match divine wisdom which can be sourced from only God. As such, we are admonished to seek wisdom from the Father of lights, who lavishes it upon His children without castigating them for submitting to Him fully.

Solomon understood this, and it didn't take long for the knowledge of his wisdom to spread beyond Israel. This is a blank cheque that godly leaders must never treat with contempt. When Jesus said no Christian can do nothing outside of Him, He really meant it.

For specifics, you cannot lead aright minus the wisdom of God. For your sake, Jesus is called the Wisdom and Power of God. Latch onto this generous gift—ask God to grant you the wisdom to manifest His will on earth through purposeful leadership.

- ⬦ 202 -

THE SOURCE OF TEMPTATION

"But each person is tempted when they
are dragged away by their own evil desire and enticed.
Then, after desire has conceived, it gives birth to sin; and sin,
when it is full-grown, gives birth to death."
James 1:14, 15, NIV

The Bible makes where temptations emerge obvious. This indicates that temptations are neither superimposed on us nor by accident. Here, Scripture reveals that temptations rear their ugly heads through the enticement—an attraction—Like a womb that no longer has the capacity to hold a fully developed baby, the womb of a man's heart births sin at the fully-developed stage. But it doesn't stop there: just like a baby that still needs to grow after birth through adequate nutrition, the full-grown stage of the sin birthed, after it has been fed, is death!

This should make us understand the importance of being purged by the supremacy of Scripture backed by the power of God's Spirit. Whenever you see anyone caught in an undesirable act, you must understand that they didn't just make that decision overnight. They actually have made that decision over and over again through the desires they kept nurturing in their heart. A leader who is able to avoid being dragged away by his desire won't bear sin that will lead to eternal death (separation from the Father). Leaders must be careful never to allow their offices to become a smokescreen that encourages evil.

- ◻ 203 -

TAME YOUR EMOTIONS

*"My dear brothers and sisters, take note of this:
Everyone should be quick to listen, slow to speak
and slow to become angry, because human anger
does not produce the righteousness that God desires."*
James 1:19, 20, NIV

This gem above has saved many people from making the wrong decisions and saying regrettable things! As a leader, we have been admonished to be quick to listen because doing so meticulously helps us to understand every situation well, including the subtle details. It is also a demonstration of self-control because we are often, if not always, tempted to talk when we should listen.

We are also admonished to be slow to speak; this does not indicate slurred speech. Rather, the emphasis is on exercising caution to ensure effective communication through words that are seasoned with salt. You are being slow to speak because you don't want to make damaging utterances.

Finally, we must be slow to anger because it is a manifestation of the flesh, and no man can act righteously whenever anger grips them. The work of the flesh cannot birth the fruit of the Spirit.

- 204 -

FAVOURITISM

"My brothers and sisters, believers in our glorious
Lord Jesus Christ must not show favoritism."
James 2:1, NIV

Favouritism is the practice of giving unfair preferential treatment to one person or group at the expense of another. Believers in Christ must acknowledge that God is fair in all His dealings, and He expects us to emulate Him. Exhibiting favouritism causes the neglected party to feel discriminated against and powerless. It could make them battle with low self-esteem. It will dent their morale, creating a toxic atmosphere of unhealthy competition and resentment among individuals.

For this reason, godly leaders should avoid favouritism like the plague. It is a misrepresentation of God's decision to judge all men righteously on the last day. By contrast, it gladdens the Lord when we treat all men with fairness or never give anyone undue advantage over others.

- 🔷 205 -

TAME YOUR TONGUE

*"Likewise, the tongue is a small part of the body,
but it makes great boasts. Consider what a great forest
is set on fire by a small spark. The tongue also is a fire,
a world of evil among the parts of the body. It corrupts
the whole body, sets the whole course of one's life on fire,
and is itself set on fire by hell. All kinds of animals,
birds, reptiles and sea creatures are being tamed and
have been tamed by mankind, but no human being
can tame the tongue. It is a restless evil,
full of deadly poison."*
James 3:5-7, NIV

*"For, 'Whoever would love life and see good days
must keep their tongue from evil and their
lips from deceitful speech.'"*
1 Peter 3:10, NIV

This book has emphasized the importance of ensuring that our utterances are powered by grace, and these portions of Scripture give further credence. Although small, the tongue makes great boasts if not reined in. Though it appears harmless, Scripture submits that it can set one's life on fire—it can lead to destruction—and, worse still, cause one to go to hell!

The further disclosure that no human can tame the tongue is proof that godly leaders need God's help, through His life-giving Spirit, to always make edifying, reassuring and transforming utterances. The importance of keeping one's tongue in check is solidified by the second portion of Scripture. You cannot make evil utterances and expect to see good days because good and evil don't co-exist in the same space.

Godly leaders must, therefore, pay full attention to this very potent organ that can make or break not just their leadership, but also their very lives. We preserve our tongues from telling lies, making vain boasts and cursing people—even when they truly hurt us—by submitting to the Spirit whose fruit empowers us to lead victorious lives.

– 206 –

SELFISH AMBITION

"For where you have envy and selfish ambition,
there you find disorder and every evil practice."
James 3:16, NIV

Simply put, disorder and evil practices are born out of envy and selfish ambition. Therefore, any sign of these evil twins (envy and selfish ambition) must be quickly discerned and tackled. They are inseparably linked because envy motivates one to seek one's self-interest alone. Consequently, one will have to battle disorder which is a state of confusion or something that disrupts the systematic functioning of a structure, thus making a mockery of one's efforts.

A godly leader must rid himself and others of selfish ambition because it turns individuals from servants of God into servant of themselves. The Greek word for selfishness is "eritheia" which means a desire to put oneself forward. Christians don't entertain selfish ambition because, in all humility, we consider others more significant than ourselves.

- ◻ 207 -

THE SOURCE OF FIGHTS AND QUARRELS

"What causes fights and quarrels among you?
Don't they come from your desires that battle within you?
You desire but do not have, so you kill. You covet
but you cannot get what you want, so you quarrel and fight.
You do not have because you do not ask God."
James 4:1, 2, NIV

Fights and quarrels which are a mainstay of some humans' lives do not occur by accident. The Bible reveals that they emerge from our desires that battle within us. In other words, avoidable quarrels and fights are a function of the evil desires men nurse over time, including covetousness.

When men desire something, but they do not have it, they resort to killing which may be physical, mental or emotional. This gem simply reveals the right path godly leaders should tread when they have a genuine need: asking God to meet their needs instead of coveting what belongs to others.

- 💎 208 -

FRIENDSHIP WITH THE WORLD

"You adulterous people, don't you know
that friendship with the world means enmity against God?
Therefore, anyone who chooses to be a friend of
the world becomes an enemy of God."
James 4:4, NIV

Whether or not we ignore this fact, the world is a place of temptation. Even Jesus was shown the glory of the world by the tempter, and it was offered to Him in exchange for worship. Many godly leaders will struggle in their walk with God because of their friendship with the world. They have failed to realize that there is no middle ground in God's Kingdom. You cannot serve God and money at the same. Similarly, you cannot be friends with God and embrace the allure of the world simultaneously. It is either you are God's friend and consequently the world's enemy or God's enemy and subsequently the world's friend.

Enmity is a state or feeling of active opposition or hostility. When godly leaders embrace the offerings of the world—its philosophies, mindsets and lifestyles—they automatically announce their opposition to God, which can only lead to shame and destruction. This is why Scripture affirms that though we temporarily live "in" the world, we are not "of" the world. Christians, including godly leaders, do not function by the world's modus operandi.

There is no demilitarization zone when it comes to the all-out war between heaven and hell. As a godly leader, therefore, you must really ascertain whether you are on the Lord's side, or you are giving room for the devil to advance his cause.

- ◎ 209 -

AVOID SLANDER AND JUDGEMENT

"Brothers and sisters, do not slander
one another. Anyone who speaks against a brother
or sister or judges them speaks against the law
and judges it. When you judge the law, you are not
keeping it, but sitting in judgment on it."
James 4:11, NIV

If truth be told, this is an offshoot of keeping one's mouth from speaking evil. The very action or crime of making a false spoken statement that has the potential to damage a person's reputation is slander. Sadly, it has found its way into everyday life. It is even sadder that some believers indulge in it without considering its far-reaching consequences. The Bible clearly forbids slander and wrong judgement.

What is more, godly leaders must understand that slander and unfair judgement can occur internally (in the heart) and verbally. And the God who clearly sees the heart won't judge you less because you don't vocalize what you actually harbour.

James makes us understand that pointing an accusing finger at a fellow believer counters the law, for there is only one Law Giver and Judge: Jesus Christ. When godly leaders speak against fellow brethren, we expose a judgemental attitude and a superiority complex that dishonour the Lord. If you don't want to be judged, don't judge others falsely as well.

- ◻ 210 -

BOASTING

"Now listen, you who say, "Today or tomorrow
we will go to this or that city, spend a year there,
carry on business and make money." Why, you do not
even know what will happen tomorrow. What is your life?
You are a mist that appears for a little while and then vanishes.
Instead, you ought to say, 'If it is the Lord's will, we will
live and do this or that.' As it is, you boast in your
arrogant schemes. All such boasting is evil.
If anyone, then, knows the good they ought to do
and doesn't do it, it is sin for them."
James 4:13-17, NIV

Whenever an individual talks with excessive pride and self-satisfaction about their achievements, possessions or abilities, it is said to be a boast. Many leaders are outright boastful, and godly leaders must never be cut from the same material. To speak boastfully is to act as though you know what will happen in the future—even if it is a second from now!

Many leaders have uttered and made boastful plans which have amounted to nothing because of their failure to constantly ask themselves one question: what is your life? Godly leaders must understand that they are mists that appear for a little while and then vanish. No one will dwell on earth forever.

Therefore, instead of making vain boasts, simply surrender your ability to execute ideas to the will of God. This is how to walk in the reality that the builder will build in vain unless the Lord first builds the house and remain humble because of the temporariness of life.

- 211 -

RICH OPPRESSORS

*"Now listen, you rich people, weep and wail
because of the misery that is coming on you.
Your wealth has rotted, and moths have eaten your clothes.
Your gold and silver are corroded. Their corrosion will testify
against you and eat your flesh like fire. You have hoarded
wealth in the last days. Look! The wages you failed
to pay the workers who mowed your fields are crying
out against you. The cries of the harvesters have
reached the ears of the Lord Almighty.
You have lived on earth in luxury and self-indulgence.
You have fattened yourselves in the day of slaughter.
You have condemned and murdered the innocent one,
who was not opposing you."
James 5:3, NIV*

The riches that leadership attracts have sadly been deployed as a tool of oppression by ungodly leaders. God frowns upon the deeds of such people because the cries of the oppressed have reached His ears. Although these oppressors have lived in luxury, they are actually headed for doom!

Godly leaders must understand that riches are tools given to advance God's agenda. Never should wealth become a scorpion's tail or a whip that is used for selfish reasons. Godly leaders don't go on expensive holidays or flaunt ostentatious lifestyles when their employees have yet to be paid their wages or salaries. Godly leaders don't reduce their employees' wages arbitrarily as Laban did to Jacob. Rich oppressors don't glorify God, and He will judge them accordingly.

- ❑ 212 -

AVOID SWEARING

"Above all, my brothers and sisters, do not swear
—not by heaven or by earth or by anything else.
All you need to say is a simple 'Yes' or 'No.'
Otherwise you will be condemned."
James 5:12, NIV

Some people are tempted to add another layer of authenticity to what they have said by swearing to God. They believe this piques the interest of their listeners. The Bible says otherwise, though: godly leaders are instructed not to swear by anything.

Since we are the children of the God whose words don't return to Him void, our "yes" or "no" should be enough. We should refrain from indulging in any form of religiosity that misrepresents God.

- 🔲 213 -

TROUBLE AND HAPPINESS

"Is anyone among you in trouble? Let them pray.
Is anyone happy? Let them sing songs of praise."
James 5:13, NIV

By now, godly leaders understand that leadership isn't a smooth journey all through. There will be days of unbridled joy and days one will have to endure trials. The Bible, therefore, teaches godly leaders how to approach both seasons.

In times of trouble, we are expected to seek God's intervention by praying to Him. During the season of happiness, we ought to praise Him passionately. Both situations show that there is no excuse not to commune with God at all times. When godly leaders employ these heaven-approved approaches, divine outcomes that strengthen such leaders are birthed.

THE BOOK OF
I PETER

- 💎 214 -

REVERENT FEAR

*"Since you call on a Father who judges each
person's work impartially, live out your time
as foreigners here in reverent fear."*
I Peter 1:17, NIV

At this juncture of this book, it shouldn't come as a surprise that God is an impartial Judge. For this reason, godly leaders must live on earth as foreigners with reverent fear of God. As foreigners, we mustn't conform to the customs of this world, and we must be conscious of our ultimate heavenly home when all is said and done.

The gem speaks about godly leaders living, not in irrational fear, but the fear that deeply respects God and acknowledges Him as a consuming Fire that judges the works of every man. Beyond seeing Him as our heavenly Father who meets our needs, we know Him as the Judge who will never withhold His rod of discipline when it should be administered.

- 💎 215 -

RID YOURSELF OF GREMLINS

*"Therefore, rid yourselves of all malice and all deceit,
hypocrisy, envy, and slander of every kind."*
I Peter 2:1, NIV

According to Hollywood, gremlins may be described as a horde of malevolently mischievous monsters that go on to cause great harm and destruction by getting inside things, especially machines, to make them stop working. In this book, the importance of ridding oneself of anything that isn't consistent with the character of the Holy Spirit cannot be overemphasized.

Here, Apostle Peter is admonishing godly leaders to rid themselves of some gremlins that encourage self-centredness. The first is malice which is described as ill-will or a desire to cause pain, injury, or distress to another person.

The second is deceit which is intentional dishonesty achieved by concealing or misrepresenting the truth. Hypocrisy which entails holding others up to standards that we don't uphold is the third. This refers to leaders who talk the talk without walking the talk. Envy is the fourth, and we can describe it as a resentful discontent towards someone who possesses something that we crave.

Finally, we have slander which has been discussed in a previous gem—using false or misleading words to harm another person's reputation. Putting away these gremlins that cause leaders to malfunction will mean putting our self-interest away and seeking the well-being of others, thus fostering mutually beneficial relationships.

- 💎 216 -

INNER BEAUTY

*"Your beauty should not come from outward
adornment, such as elaborate hairstyles and the wearing
of gold jewelry or fine clothes. Rather, it should be that
of your inner self, the unfading beauty of a gentle and
quiet spirit, which is of great worth in God's sight."*
I Peter 3:4, NIV

The outlandish display of outward adornment is something associated with a number of leaders, but this gem teaches us that our beauty should not come from such outward adornment that includes elaborate hairstyles, wearing of gold jewellery or even fine clothes. Make no mistake about this, please: the Bible doesn't condemn the use of clothing and clothing accessories as long as they are used moderately or decently.

Although this Scripture originally addressed the Christian women of that time, it is applicable to godly leaders, too.

Hence, godly leaders are expected to focus more on their inner selves where true, permanent beauty lies. This beauty of a gentle and quiet spirit is held in high esteem by God. The importance of tending more to our inner parts cannot be overemphasized because it ultimately determines what we do outwardly.

- 💎 217 -

YOUR GIFTS ARE FOR SERVICE

"Each of you should use whatever gift you have received to serve others, as faithful stewards of God's grace in its various forms."
I Peter 4:10, NIV

This is a timely reminder. With the consciousness that there is nothing a man owns unless it is first given by God, we shouldn't use our gifts for show-off, indulgence in unhealthy rivalry or, as we have seen before, the oppression of our subordinates. Godly leaders must appreciate the fact that they are stewards and must be faithful in the exercise of their duties. As a steward, you are simply managing the property (resources) of your Master, God, until His Second Coming.

This reality should provoke us unto humility and selfless service. We should serve others knowing full well that God, who cannot be stranded, could easily have chosen other people in place of us. Although there may be fringe benefits of service, the major focus is still on faithful and selfless service.

- 💎 218 -

BE ALERT AND SOBER

"Be alert and of sober mind.
Your enemy the devil prowls around like
a roaring lion looking for someone to devour."
I Peter 5:8, NIV

The knowledge of the adversary should put any godly leader in offensive or defensive mode to tackle issues that arise. Just like a soldier, godly leaders are expected to be battle-ready for whatever hostility that may arise from the devil's camp. We are also expected to be sober-minded; this makes us reflective, humble and receptive to much-needed change. A sober leader will most likely be a more empathetic and much wiser person.

According to Apostle Peter, our sobriety and alertness should be targeted at neutralizing the plans of the enemy who seeks whom to devour. When we study a lion, we see how it patiently observes its prey before exploiting the prey's weakness. Godly leaders must not give the devil a foothold through shortcomings like sin, laziness and mismanagement of resources.

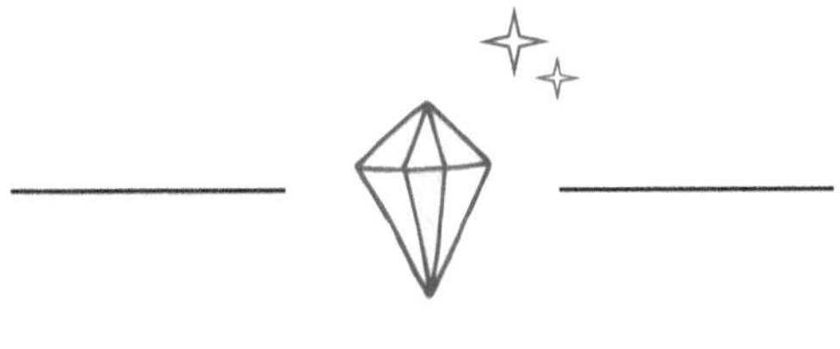

THE BOOK OF
II PETER

- ◈ 219 -

GROWING IN KNOWLEDGE

*"For this very reason, make every effort to add
to your faith goodness; and to goodness, knowledge;
and to knowledge, self-control; and to self-control,
perseverance; and to perseverance, godliness;
and to godliness, mutual affection; and to mutual affection,
love. For if you possess these qualities in increasing measure,
they will keep you from being ineffective and unproductive
in your knowledge of our Lord Jesus Christ."*
II Peter 1:7, 8, NIV

Godly leaders should be examples of productivity and effectiveness, but how do we attain this level of maturity? This gem unveils how we can grow in the knowledge of Jesus Christ for productivity and effectiveness.

First, the Bible encourages us to make every effort to add goodness to our faith. The Easton's Bible Dictionary defines goodness not as a mere passive quality, but the deliberate preference of right to wrong, the firm and persistent resistance of all moral evil, and the choosing and following of all moral good.

The next quality we are encouraged to add to this is knowledge. Knowledge refers to the facts, information, and skills that are acquired by a person through experience or education. Godly leaders, therefore, must be seekers of not just any knowledge, but that which benefits our walk with, and work for, God. To strengthen this layer is the need to add self-control. Self-control is defined as the ability to regulate one's emotions, thoughts and behaviour in the face of temptations and impulses; the absence of this quality in any leader will lead to eventual destruction.

Apostle Peter, on top of self-control, speaks of perseverance which is persistence in doing something despite the difficulty or delay in achieving success. Godliness is the next required trait; it is the manifestation of God's attributes and character through man. An ungodly leader will eventually know ruin. The next quality is brotherly kindness which reveals mutual affection, concern and connectedness among believers. Closely tied to the apron of mutual affection is the most important of all qualities: love. There isn't a better definition of love than what obtains in First Corinthians 13. It is patient and kind, it doesn't envy or boast, it is not arrogant or rude, it doesn't insist on its own, it is not irritable or resentful and it rejoices at the truth, not wrongdoing.

When a godly leader possesses these qualities in increasing measure, unproductivity and ineffectiveness will be far from them.

~ ◈ 220 ~

WHAT HAS MASTERED YOU

"They promise them freedom, while they themselves
are slaves of depravity—for 'people are slaves
to whatever has mastered them.'"
II Peter 2:19, NIV

You probably have heard a narrative about how one scandal or allegation spelt the beginning of the downfall of a leader brimming with huge prospects. This sadly happens when such a leader has chosen to remain a slave to ungodly attributes. Of course, this is not God's original design for anyone. The gem here reveals that people are slaves to whatever has mastered them. Recall that mastery takes time, meaning that people become enslaved by any form of depravity they have given the appropriate environment to thrive.

As a godly leader, therefore, sincerely ask yourself this question: who and what have mastered me? In the light of this, whatever or whoever you have idolized over time must be dealt with so that only God can be enthroned in your life.

THE BOOK OF
I JOHN

- 💎 221 -

LOVE NOT THE WORLD

"Do not love the world or anything in the world.
If anyone loves the world, love for the Father is not in them.
For everything in the world—the lust of the flesh, the lust
of the eyes, and the pride of life—comes not from the Father
but from the world. The world and its desires pass away,
but whoever does the will of God lives forever."
I John 2:15-17, NIV

This treasure trove of a book has taught godly leaders about the importance of non-conformity to the world, which is further buttressed by Scripture above. Love for the world and its offerings is automatically hatred for God. The world's offerings are broadly categorized into the lust of the flesh, the lust of the eyes and the pride of life. These gratify the flesh to the detriment of your spirit and soul. The lust of the flesh includes sexual immorality, gluttony and excessive comfort that extinguishes productivity.

The lust of the eyes is the sinful desire to possess whatever we see that is appealing without caring to know whether or not God wants us to have it. The pride of life simply encompasses pride in one's attainments and possessions. This happens when a leader forgets that they are who they are only by the grace of Jesus. King Nebuchadnezzer was guilty of this, and God banished him from human society. The rich fool who gloried in what he had gathered died that very night! These narratives are proof that God truly resists the proud.

Godly leaders should steer clear of these manifestations of worldliness if they are indeed intentional about representing God correctly.

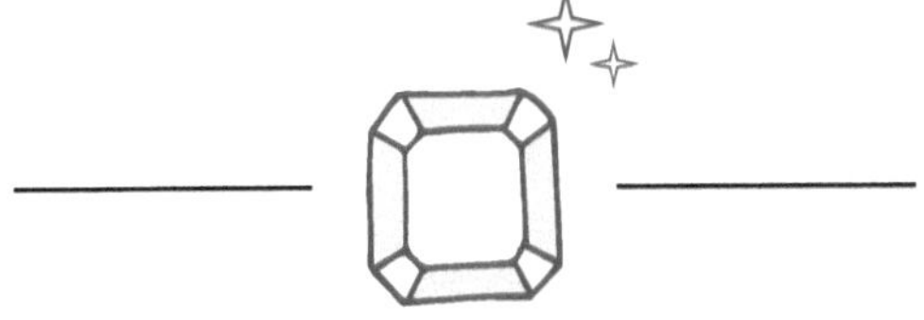

THE BOOK OF
REVELATION

- 222 -

LEADERS ARE ACCOUNTABLE

"Write, therefore, what you have seen,
what is now and what will take place later.
The mystery of the seven stars that you saw in
my right hand and of the seven golden lampstands
is this: The seven stars are the angels of the seven churches,
and the seven lampstands are the seven churches."
Revelation 1:19, 20, NIV

One of the realities that stood out for me in the first chapter of Revelation is the inevitability of being accountable as far as leadership is concerned. Beyond the first chapter, letters were written to the seven churches in Asia: Ephesus, Smyrna, Pergamum, Thyatira, Sardis, Philadelphia and Laodicea.

One common theme in all the letters is accountability, as Jesus praised, rebuked and warned members of the seven churches as deemed necessary. Godly leaders must always walk in the realization that they are accountable to God just like the led are accountable to them.

- ◻ 223 -

HOSTILE ENVIRONMENT

*"I know where you live—where Satan has his throne.
Yet you remain true to my name. You did not renounce
your faith in me, not even in the days of Antipas,
my faithful witness, who was put to death in
your city—where Satan lives."*
Revelation 2:13, NIV

Here, the church in Pergamum was commended for remaining faithful to God despite being present where Satan's throne existed. They didn't waver in the faith even when one of them, Antipas, was martyred. Similarly, many godly leaders will find themselves in hostile environments, and they are expected to shine their lights there.

They should do this with the consciousness that God will not put on anyone more than they can bear, and His commandments, by the help of the Spirit, are not burdensome. godly leaders are expected to remain faithful and steadfast come what may.

- 224 -

LEADERS MUST NOT BE LUKEWARM

*"So, because you are lukewarm—neither hot nor cold
—I am about to spit you out of my mouth."*
Revelation 3:16, NIV

A letter was written to the church in Laodicea which was a very prosperous Phrygian city that had economic sectors which were well known in the then ancient world, from banking, wool and medicinal product industries.

The Laodicean church had allowed worldly prosperity to dull their spirits, thus they became lukewarm. They became indifferent to the purposes and pleasures of God. In the same vein, when a leader is lukewarm, they do things with little enthusiasm or half-heartedly. No lukewarm leader fulfils their potential, and this will have a negative impact on those connected to them.

If we will go by the Bible's analogy, godly leaders should be "hot", exuding zeal, confidence, wisdom and energy with which to execute divine mandate. Jesus was clear about spitting lukewarm people out of His mouth; in other words, He will sever His relationship with them because they have chosen not to do His bidding anymore.

- ◎ 225 -

SOME REVELATIONS ARE FOR PERSONAL CONSUMPTION

*"And when the seven thunders spoke,
I was about to write; but I heard a voice from
heaven say, 'Seal up what the seven thunders
have said and do not write it down.'"*
Revelation 10:4, NIV

One of the hallmarks of exemplary leadership is the ability to discern sensitive information that should be kept close to your chest and should not get to the public domain like John did in Scripture above, under divine instruction. The mismanagement of such information can lead to serious crisis for the leaders and the led.

So, while your office may attract privileged information, godly leaders must leverage maturity, as exercised through self-control, to handle the disclosure. You should speak only when necessary and keep quiet when God instructs you to do so.

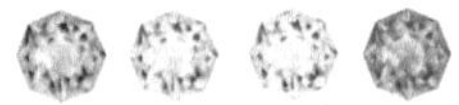

THE AUTHOR

Chris Omoijiade, affectionately known as the CEO, is a dynamic figure whose multifaceted talents have left an indelible mark across diverse professional spheres. As an entrepreneur, engaging speaker, dedicated mentor, insightful coach, and innovative consultant, and minister, Chris' passion for teaching leadership and personal success principles has been the driving force behind his illustrious career.

He serves as the Chief Storyteller and Executive at TCOC Global, a boutique consulting firm dedicated to implementing effective tools for enhancing the value proposition and productivity of individuals and businesses. With over two decades of experience, Chris has conducted impactful trainings for prestigious entities such as Continental RE, Diamonds and Pearls, Etisalat, the Nigerian Army, Zapphaire Events, Corona Schools, and Wole Olanipekun & Co., among others, both in Nigeria and internationally.

Chris' expertise spans management consulting, corporate training, and legal services. He earned himself a Bachelor of Laws degree from the University of Lagos and a

Master of Law in Telecommunications and Maritime Law from the University of Hertfordshire, UK. His skill set includes leadership coaching, personal effectiveness, success principles, strategic planning, people management consultancy, and emotional intelligence, catering to diverse clients locally and internationally.

In addition to his professional pursuits, Chris is a minister and a proud graduate of the Koinonia School of Ministry in Abuja. He holds a diploma in Theology and Ministry from the Remnants Christian Network-Adullam in Makurdi, Benue state. Active in esteemed professional bodies like the Nigerian Bar Association, International Bar Association, Institute of Directors, and Chartered Institute of Arbitrators, Chris is dedicated to both professional and spiritual growth.

Chris' literary contributions include insightful books such as 'Get Ahead: Practical Steps to Face Life's Realities and Embrace Success,' 'The Irrefutable Role of Gatekeepers,' and the recently concluded 'You Too Can Be Debt Free.' This latest work stands as a testament to Chris' personal journey as a debt survivor, reflecting his passionate commitment to empowering others in their financial freedom and journey into becoming the wealthy man whom God has designed them to be.

As the pioneer of Arimathea Believers Network, Chris envisions a ministry that raises and empowers apostles in the marketplace to seek and fulfill God's will. His desire to unleash the authority and power of God within the marketplace underscores his commitment to righteous apostles influencing and transforming the business landscape.

Happily married with two sons, Chris calls Lagos, Nigeria, home. His unwavering commitment to professional excellence and holistic development is evident in his active involvement in various professional associations, where he continues to contribute his expertise and leadership.

To book Chris for your speaking engagements, consulting, company keynote addresses, trainings, and for ministrations, you can use any of the channels below:

📞 +234 908 123 0000

✉ admin@tcocglobal.com
✉ Chris@chrisomoijiade.com
✉ Ceo@tcocglobal.com

Follow on social media

▶ chrisomoijiade

⊙ chrisomoijiade
⊙ @tcocglobal
⊙ @arimathea_believers_network

✕ chrisomoijiade

in christopher Omoijiade
in The Chris Omoijiade Company

🌐 www.chrisomoijiade.com
🌐 www.tcocglobal.com
🌐 www.arimatheanetwork.org

♪ comoijiade